For Reference

Not to be taken from this room

HOW IT STARTED

HOW IT STARTED

Webb Garrison

Illustrated by Charles Cox

ABINGDON PRESS • Nashville and New York

HOW IT STARTED

Copyright © 1972 by Abingdon Press

ISBN 0-687-17605-0

Library of Congress Catalog Card Number: 72-173951

MANUFACTURED BY THE PARTHENON PRESS AT
NASHVILLE, TENNESSEE, UNITED STATES OF AMERICA

TO

Cindy, Beth, Pat, Carol, and Meredith
whose curiosity won't let Grand get rusty
and Webb III who's just getting started

PREFACE

Through the influence of tradition we do some things so habitually we hardly recognize what we are doing. As a result of dreams, sudden hunches, and pure luck, individual men and women have enriched the lives of all posterity. By means of converging social influences in which individual contributions have been so minor that no traces can be found, the course of civilization has been altered.

Addressed to readers of every age and background who have little in common except curiosity, this nontechnical volume seeks to answer a great many questions about the how, when, and why of things.

To serve its purpose fully, it must also whet curiosity—sending readers to seek more details about matters treated here and to inquire about origins of other things not so much as mentioned.

While it is my confident hope that this brief book will fill a much-used spot on the reference shelf of many a library, it is in no sense an academic work. Hopefully, it will yield as much fun as information. Ideally, it will prove so good a conversation starter that readers can't resist sending copies to relatives and friends who "have everything."

To all who share the high adventure of discovering and of knowing, the author wishes, "Happy hunting!"

Webb Garrison

CONTENTS

Good Luck—and Bad

FRIDAY THE THIRTEENTH

Two long and tangled chains of circumstance led to the elevation of Friday the thirteenth as first among the ominous days.

In some ancient cultures Friday was regarded as lucky. Early Christians rejected this idea. Jesus was crucified on Friday, they pointed out. At the moment of his death the powers of evil were at the height of their influence in heaven as well as on earth. Consequently, Friday was the most fearful day of the week. If demons and workers of evil were on the prowl, intended victims ran greater risk on Friday than on such ordinary days as Monday and Thursday.

No one knows how long the number thirteen has been considered unlucky. At least as early as the time of Greek philosophers who thought they found mathematical relationships permeating the universe, the odd number was frowned upon. Unlike such numbers as four and twelve, it has no divisors. Both one and three are "perfect" numbers—flawlessly symmetrical when represented by dots—but thirteen is grotesque and misshapen. There is no way to arrange thirteen dots in a completely orderly pattern.

Taken alone, either Friday or the thirteenth of the month was a time of special danger. When the two coincided to yield Friday the thirteenth, sensible persons took all possible precautions and absolutely refused to launch new enterprises. So elevated in popular thought, the dreadful day is still widely regarded as being at least a bit more sinister than any other.

11

RIGHT SIDE OF THE BED

Though seldom taken seriously these days, for many centuries even educated and literate persons considered it important to start the day by getting out of bed on the right side.

The meaning of the verbal formula, which is now more familiar than the ceremony that produced it, is literal. To get out of bed on the left side was to invite trouble, for the left side (Latin *sinister*) provided easy access for evil spirits.

It wasn't enough to get out on the right, or the side of good luck. Cautious persons were careful about the way they placed their feet on the floor. Right foot foremost was the rule; to get up on the right side of the bed but to place one's left foot on the floor first was likely to make a person cross all day!

RABBIT'S FOOT

Though native to Europe, the wild rabbit never became so prominent as the hare on that continent. Introduced into the New World by early settlers, the rabbit found an environment just right for it and as a result flourished from the start.

Hunters found it hard to see small animals of nearly uniform brown color, and trappers discovered that rabbits are adept at stealing bait without being caught. Many frontier yarns and folktales glorified the supposed wisdom of the rabbit.

Since rabbits were much harder to get than many kinds of game, the hunter or trapper who outsmarted the little animal was prone to boast about it. To prove the truth of his story he had to exhibit a part of the animal as a trophy. Tails and ears were sometimes used for this purpose, but feet proved far more satisfactory.

Elevated to importance in this fashion, the foot of the animal that often eludes its foes came to be taken as a good luck charm. This custom that was born on the American frontier later crossed the Atlantic from west to east when enterprising Yankee merchants began exporting the feet of rabbits for sale in Europe.

WISH ON A STAR

To the ancients a falling star (or meteorite) was considered a bad omen. It was a sure sign of quarreling among the gods or of wrath on the part of some deity who was angry with mankind.

In order to counteract the influence of this ominous sign, it was necessary to repeat very rapidly a complex verbal formula before the falling star disappeared or hit the earth. Numerous protective patterns were devised and used by a variety of peoples.

Long after the reason for repeating memorized lines lost its vitality, the formulas themselves were transmitted orally from generation to generation. Since good luck followed the successful repetition of a semimagical saying, it was an easy transition for early Englishmen to devise a new set of lines attesting to the power of a wish on a star.

> Star light, star bright
> First star I've seen tonight;
> I wish I may, I wish I might
> Have the wish I wish tonight.

Repeated rapidly without error immediately after catching the first glimpse of a star, these words are sure to bring good luck!

FOUR-LEAF CLOVER

Association of good luck with a four-leaf clover is so widespread and so old that documentary evidence about its beginning cannot be found.

Many scholars assert that its resemblance to the cross on which Jesus died elevated the four-leaf clover into prominence.

Seeking to account for the good luck they considered to be associated with this plant, European peasants concocted an elaborate legend. According to it, four-leaf clovers were common in the Garden of Eden. On her expulsion from paradise, Eve hastily grabbed one and took it with her as a reminder of earlier bliss.

This tale, unfortunately, is comparatively modern in origin. Instead of explaining how the four-leaf clover came to be a symbol of good luck, the legend is a product of the prevailing attitude toward the plant.

Even the superficial resemblance to the cross isn't fully adequate as an explanation for the high regard with which four-leaf clovers have been held in non-Christian cultures. More than any other factor, rarity probably contributed to attitudes about it. Anything that is out of the ordinary is likely to be prized, hence associated with beneficent influences.

In the case of the four-leaf clover, the plant that reminds the pious of Jesus' cross had two powerful assets: rarity plus symbolism.

BLACK CAT

Black is the color of night, when the life-giving sun has withdrawn its presence. Association of black with evil forces was therefore logical and inevitable.

The cat is the most mysterious of domestic animals, credited with ability to see in the dark and so agile that it was long considered to have nine lives instead of one.

Small wonder, therefore, that in medieval lore many a tale stressed the fact that Satan likes to assume the form of a black cat. This association with the demonic caused any black cat, however tame, to be called a "familiar"—or companion of the Evil One.

Prudent folk didn't like to keep black cats about the household and often killed kittens whose markings indicated they were potential "familiars." This meant that a person might go for months or years without seeing a black cat; when he did, he took the animal's appearance as an omen of impending crisis or tragedy.

When a black cat crossed the roadway in front of a person, on foot or in a horsedrawn vehicle, this was considered a warning to turn around and go home. Even today a few ultracautious persons detour in order to avoid going along a street across which one of Satan's feline representatives has just strolled.

THIRTEEN AT TABLE

Measured by any standard, history's most famous meal is the Last Supper, Jesus' last meal before his betrayal and arrest —eaten in the company of his twelve disciples. The presence of a traitor among the celebrants, plus fateful and dramatic events both at the table and immediately afterward, branded the meal itself as potent with bad luck.

The impact of scripture's verbal account was strengthened by literally hundreds of different paintings and drawings showing the fateful feast.

Until comparatively recent times, few Westerners would consent to sit at a table around which thirteen persons were gathered.

Early in the nineteenth century a few celebrated persons defied the ancient prohibition and deliberately arranged dinner parties for thirteen persons. One of the most celebrated of these affairs was held by English poet and critic Matthew Arnold. Newspapers devoted a great deal of space to the dinner at which Arnold thumbed his nose at fate—and hence prepared the public to react emotionally when the critic died within a year after the meal.

Later a brief flurry of Thirteen Clubs flourished in New

York, where men and women determined to defy the superstition regularly ate in groups of thirteen. For the most part, though, today's hostesses are likely to go to considerable pains to avoid having a luncheon or dinner at which a table is surrounded by the same number of persons who participated in the Last Supper.

HORSESHOE OVER THE DOOR

Legend credits St. Dunstan with having given the horseshoe its potency.

According to old stories, the blacksmith saint was one day approached by a man who lifted one of his own feet and asked for service. Dunstan instantly recognized him as the Devil.

Pretending obedience, the saint succeeded in tying the Devil to the wall before shoeing his cloven hoofs. He deliberately made the job so painful that the Devil roared for mercy. Dunstan refused to release him until he gave his solemn oath never to enter a place where he saw a horseshoe displayed!

Actually, veneration for the horseshoe is much older than the traditional story that seeks to explain it. The horseshoe unites within itself three lucky elements: it is made of iron, it is associated with horses, and it is crescent-shaped. With such a combination, it could not fail to be a protector of the household—or so medieval folk reasoned.

Enlightenment associated with the coming of modern times didn't demolish the inherited views about the horseshoe's power. As late as 1805 when Lord Horatio Nelson prepared to meet his nation's foes in the Battle of Trafalgar, the cautious Englishman ceremonially nailed a horseshoe to the mast of his command ship *Victory*.

ROBIN REDBREAST

One of the most colorful birds of Europe and America is so versatile that it is considered a harbinger of good news—or of bad, depending upon the circumstances.

Appearance of a robin, linked with the coming of spring, is widely regarded as a sign that a wish will be fulfilled. But many persons regard the bird as a harbinger of death. Both notions are rooted in ancient veneration for birds of all kinds. Because it is colorful, the robin was particularly prized.

One story explains the bird's red breast by saying that when Jesus was on his way to Calvary a robin picked a thorn out of his crown. A drop of blood from the Savior's head touched the little creature who was trying to ease his misery and left him perpetually marked with red.

Especially in Germany and Austria, folktales linked the robin with death. In ballad form the famous story of "The Babes in the Wood" has Robin Redbreast piously covering the pretty pair with leaves after the lost children die.

Small wonder that many persons who considered it good luck to catch a glimpse of the harbinger of spring were reluctant to kill or to keep a robin. An English analyst of customs, writing about a century ago, discounted the whole business. "The plain truth is," said T. Sharper Knowlson, "that there is no more impertinent or mischievous thief in the whole tribe of feathers."

KNOCK ON WOOD

Half jestingly but half seriously, Will Rogers made it a practice always to knock on wood before undertaking a project. Numerous other noted persons of modern times have done the same thing. Most of them follow the age-old formula of precisely three knocks.

The facetious gesture of tapping one's own head after announcing the necessity of knocking on wood is a modern variant of a custom once taken quite seriously.

The power of this rite, according to some who have pondered it, stems from the fact that Jesus was crucified on a cross of wood. During the Middle Ages hardly a cathedral in Europe was without at least a splinter solemnly alleged to have come from the true cross.

Veneration of relics did not launch the custom of regarding

17

wood with awe, however. It simply reinforced a much older set of views.

Especially in northern Europe, tree worship was once practically universal. Trees furnished wood, essential for fire, which was essential to life. Besides, the sky-god often hurled his lightning bolts directly at forest giants—notably oaks. Contact with things linked with this powerful god was a good way to avert evil.

Documentary evidence is lacking, but many factors support the view that persons originally knocked on oak for good luck. As association of this wood with the god of lightning became less powerful, careful folk continued to knock on whatever type of wood was close at hand.

WALKING UNDER A LADDER

Every sensible person knows better than to risk bad luck by walking under a ladder.

Ordinary caution has been suggested as the origin of this view of ladders. Though it probably strengthened arguments against violation of the space between a ladder and the wall, caution in the usual sense of the word isn't the prime factor here.

Since a ladder leaning against a wall forms a triangle and a triangle is a symbolic reminder of the Holy Trinity, anyone who carelessly blunders through this mystical space is risking divine wrath! At least, that is the way medieval theologians argued.

Long after such ideas had been generally dismissed from thought, the ladder still played a potent and unforgettable role in English life. Condemned men about to be hanged at Tyburn, or some other notable place of execution, were required to walk under the ladder that stood against the gallows for convenience of the executioner. Anyone who walked under such a ladder in such a set of circumstances was clearly in for a spell of very bad luck!

Stemming therefore not from one but from two or three different sources, the superstitious dread linked with walking under any ladder under any circumstances has persisted long past the disappearance of the customs and ideas that gave birth to it.

SNEEZING

Use of *gesundheit* as a way of wishing good health to a person who has just sneezed is comparatively modern; other exclamations linked with what Elizabethans liked to call "sternutation" are rooted in antiquity.

According to myth Prometheus stole rays of the sun and put them in a bottle. With his loot Prometheus flew to the inanimate figure of a man; opening the bottle, he released the life-giving light. This caused Prometheus' statue to sneeze—and come to life.

This tale, and many others, witness to the reverence with which a person's breath was regarded. Rapid loss of breath, occasioned by a sneeze, creates a dangerous situation. Unless a suitable formula is used, the space formerly occupied by air may become the abode of evil spirits.

Sneezing rites, accompanied by ritualistic sayings, are found all over the world. When a Hindu sneezes, someone close to him is supposed to exclaim, "Live!" In turn the sneezer responds, "With you!"

This formula, like the English "God bless you!" and German

gesundheit, is a way of turning a potentially unlucky situation into a lucky one. Among the Greeks and Romans several phrases were used to make sure a sneeze would have a fortunate outcome. "Long may you live!" "Jupiter preserve you!" "May you enjoy good health!" and similar formulas employed the power of words to avert the possibility of dire consequences from sneezing.

MASCOT

In the former French province of Gascony every household used to have its good luck charm, or *mascotte.* Probably through influence of the rural custom, gamblers and men-about-town borrowed the title to indicate any object, symbol, or animal that brought good luck.

In the comic opera of *La Mascotte* this concept served to name messengers from the Power of Light who helped men counteract the malicious work of evil imps under command of the archfiend Agesago.

Elevated to new importance by the world-famous opera, the mascot became a familiar feature of village life and later of athletic contests.

Once an institution or a team has selected a mascot, now usually an animal such as a goat or a dog, bad luck is sure to come if the mascot is lost or stolen. Present-day backers of athletic teams seldom regard the mascot as seriously as did folk of a few generations ago, but the mascot constitutes so important and vulnerable a prize that it has to be guarded to prevent abduction on the night before a team tangles with a longtime rival.

SPILLING SALT

For at least three thousand years, and probably much longer, it has been considered bad luck to spill salt at the table.

Much of the power of salt derives from its all but universal connection with religious rites. Greeks and Romans mixed the highly prized seasoning with their sacrificial cakes. Both the descendants of Abraham and the people with whom they fought used salt in their sacred ceremonies.

The antiquity of veneration for the now common substance suggests that attempts to link bad luck with salt spilled at Jesus' Last Supper, as depicted by Leonardo da Vinci, stop far short of full explanations. There is little doubt, however, that the impact of the painting upon the modern Western world helped to preserve and to underscore the importance of age-old notions about risks associated with spilled salt.

Religious considerations aside, a very practical factor influenced the development of concepts transmitted with little change through the centuries. Salt was once rare and expensive. It was an economic catastrophe to lose a dish of it by a careless movement of one's hand.

To avert the bad luck that is invited by spilling salt, you need only throw a pinch of it over your left shoulder with the thumb and forefinger of your right hand!

TWO-DOLLAR BILL

As practically everyone in the United States knows, a two-dollar bill is a sign of bad luck.

This piece of money gained its reputation, say some tales, because of its association with the racetrack. The two-dollar bet was long the most common one laid down on horses—and many more persons lost than won. This association may have strengthened the hold of the idea that a two-dollar bill is likely to bring misfortune, but it does not fully account for it. Canadians have no superstitious awe of the two-dollar bill.

Here is a clue to the most plausible explanation for the U. S. attitude: in the United States two-dollar bills are printed in the same colors and in practically the same style as one-dollar bills; in Canada the two-dollar bill is instantly identified because it is red. Easy confusion between one-dollar bills and two-dollars bills in the United States, leading to the frequent loss of a dollar by careless handling of currency, probably laid the foundation for the belief that two-dollar bills bring bad luck.

Oral tradition holds that you will be rewarded by good luck if you tear off one corner of a two-dollar bill—and even better luck if you tear off all four.

Superstition? Not at all—just common sense. For in spite of laws making it illegal to deface or mutilate currency, the holder of a two-dollar bill with all corners torn off is practically certain to have the good luck of failing to pass it as a one-dollar bill.

AMULETS

An amulet is anything hung round one's neck, placed like a bracelet on the wrist or ankle, or otherwise attached to the body in order to counteract evil influences and to bring good luck.

Arabic *hamalet* (that which is suspended) may have given birth to the modern name. A wide variety of substances were actually hung about the necks of ancient Arabs: precious and semiprecious stones, seeds, fragments of writing, and even artifacts produced by the wearer.

Descendants of Abraham made wide use of bits of parchment with fragments of the Law of Moses written upon them; an early reference to amulets is preserved in Isaiah 3:20 (RSV).

Coral necklaces, beads, crowns of pearls, and miniature figures of gods, heroes, horses, birds, and fishes were used as amulets by Greeks and Romans. To ensure victory in combat the professional gladiator took care to select just the right amulet and to suspend it from his neck.

Far from being dead, faith in the power of amulets still thrives. One of the most obvious fruits of this faith is use of copper braclets and anklets (valued in proportion to purity of the metal) by world-famous athletes. Few professional sporting events and no Olympic competitions of recent decades have been without at least one superstar faithfully wearing a (pure!) copper amulet.

BROKEN MIRROR

Long before mirrors were manufactured of glass having a thin coat of silver on one side, it was considered a bad omen to break a looking glass.

Some of the earliest recorded objects of this sort were shallow glass bowls or dishes; filled with water, they served reasonably well to reflect images when lighting conditions were right.

It was this type of looking glass that the Greeks used in divination, fortune telling, and other occult arts. In order to know the fate of a sick person, experts with water-filled glasses practiced catoptromancy, or the interpretation of reflections.

Practically all types of mirrors, including early ones made of burnished metal, have been widely used in attempts to foresee the workings of fate or the actions of the gods. So linked with the occult, the mirror (a means of knowing things not revealed by other methods of inquiry) became endowed with semi-magical properties.

To break a mirror or looking glass, no matter what its composition, involved a risk of incurring the wrath of the gods. What is more, the seer whose only mirror was smashed had no way to look into the future. Long considered a catastrophe of the first order, the breaking of a mirror has dwindled in importance so that now it is simply a sign of bad luck.

BUCKEYE

In practically all cultural epochs, including the Space Age, persons have tended to link good luck with anything that is remarkable, mysterious, and unexplainable. This is especially the case if the object involved happens to be small enough to carry in one's pocket or purse or to wear as an amulet.

Frontiersmen who pushed into the region now known as Ohio were astounded to discover that the fruit of a native horse chestnut, *Aesculur glabra,* looks incredibly like the eye of a deer when the nut is first exposed by shrinkage of its shell.

Clearly some extraordinary power was involved in the fact that a tree could produce fruit whose shape, color, and shiny texture looked for all the world like the eye of a fine six- or ten-pronged buck.

Instantly dubbed "buckeye" in frontier speech, the mysterious nut was for generations used as a general cure-all. To avoid illness one had only to wear the wonderful talisman in a bag hung around the neck. To get good luck it helped mightily to keep a buckeye in one's pocket!

Several varieties of the horse chestnut, though botanically very closely related to the Ohio species, yield nuts that have little in common with the eyes of deer. Obviously these are of no help in the quest for good fortune and good health.

EVIL EYE

Belief that certain persons have a blighting or malignant eye capable of doing harm—or even causing death—to anyone seen by it is one of the oldest and most widespread of superstitions.

Scripture includes a very early reference to the evil eye (Proverbs 23:6 KJV). Egyptians knew the phenomenon. So did Greeks and Romans, by whom it was called *fascinum.*

Capacity to "fascinate" gave the evil eye its potency. By using it to weave a spell, the person who had an evil eye could subdue other persons or cause them to stumble into a trap that would bring disappointment, physical injury, or death.

At no time have students of the occult even approached general agreement concerning ways to identify an evil eye. Every culture—sometimes even every individual seer—had a particular "touchstone" with which to determine whether or not a person who stared intently or gave baleful glances actually possessed the evil eye.

Though people today speak of an evil eye chiefly as a figure of speech, belief in the power of a nebulous and undefined but very real evil eye still has a substantial number of followers, some of whom use charms and amulets to protect themselves from the baleful influence of such an orb.

Food and Drink

COOKBOOK

Though some persons doubt that any cookbook should be classified as literature, volumes of this sort are high on the lists of perennial best sellers.

Recipes were preserved and transmitted from pre-Christian periods. For the most part, however, a given document described just one dish. It took the development of the printing press to spawn the book made up of a collection of recipes plus household hints.

The first American cookbook, *The Compleat Housewife*, was compiled by a resident of Williamsburg, Virginia. Famous throughout the region for her skill in the kitchen, Mrs. E. Smith yielded to the "importunity of friends" and in 1736 issued her historic book.

As the title indicates, the first American book of recipes was generously larded with directions and suggestions for work outside the kitchen. Most present-day cookbooks stick reasonably close to the stove and refrigerator; a few popular ones are laced with hints about how to make housework easier and better.

BUTTERED BREAD

Common sense suggests that buttered bread was born as a result of the fact that someone found the product of churning to add flavor and daintiness to bread.

Not so, assert medical historians Samuel B. Hand and Arthur S. Kunin of the University of Vermont College of Medicine. According to them the custom was born in a time of plague and stemmed from the fertile brain of one of the most original thinkers Europe ever produced.

Nicolaus Copernicus, now remembered chiefly for his monumental discoveries in astronomy, was educated as a theologian. As Canon of the Cathedral of Frauenburg in the Prussian diocese of Ermland, Copernicus was put in charge of defending the castle of Allenstein when it was besieged early in the sixteenth century.

As a youth, the commandant of Allenstein had studied medicine. Though he did not get an M.D. degree from the University of Padua, he maintained a lively interest in the healing arts. Consequently he took personal charge when some of the men under his command developed a "plague" never specifically diagnosed.

Copernicus tried routine treatments and found them useless. He suspected a link between the illness and food available in the castle; in order to test his theory he had various groups of defenders eat special diets. Eventually bread was identified as the culprit.

In order to stop the spread of the "plague," Copernicus experimented with buttering bread. This unheard of practice not only had beneficial results; it pleased appetites so much that it quickly spread throughout Europe.

PEANUT BUTTER

Late in the 1880's a St. Louis physician was confronted by an unusual problem. One of his patients was bordering upon "protein malnutrition," but complicated stomach disorders prevented the use of then common sources of the vital substance.

In desperation the physician had one of his aides grind a quantity of roasted peanuts with mortar and pestle. When peanut oil was added to the dry mixture, it proved palatable as well as readily digestible.

As a medical innovation the preparation excited so little

27

interest that names of the physician and his patient were not recorded. News of the new food spread very slowly at first, traveling by word of mouth. Eventually it became so generally esteemed that peanut butter gave up its place on the apothecary's shelf in order to invade groceries everywhere.

BREAKFAST FOOD

Seventh-Day Adventist Ellen Gould White was passionately devoted to her religious beliefs. Some persons considered her a bit queer because she frequently had strangely vivid dreams and occasionally experienced visions comparable to those described in scripture.

One night she encountered the Lord himself in a dream. He told her that no one should eat meat, use tobacco, or drink whisky, tea, or coffee. The impact of the dream was so great that Ellen Gould White established the Health Reform Institute at Battle Creek, Michigan.

Guests were given nut croquettes in lieu of meat plus a cereal beverage as a substitute for coffee. Charles W. Post, who devised the latter, called it Postum. He also invented a dry breakfast food that he called "Elijah's Manna." Though it was tasty, the name didn't appeal to members of the general public so it was changed to Grape-Nuts.

A surgeon who spent considerable time at the sanitarium also experimented with breakfast foods. Chiefly for the benefit of a patient who had broken her false teeth, Dr. J Harvey Kellogg made crisp flakes from ground corn.

Originally marketed as aids to health, so many breakfast foods made from cereal were devised that at one time Battle Creek alone listed more than thirty manufacturers.

CANE SUGAR

Until modern times honey was the only sweetening agent generally available to Europeans.

Spanish explorers in the New World were keenly interested

in a kind of native cane whose juice was sweet, but no one quite knew what to do with it. That situation changed with the discovery of native methods for making rum from it.

A party of Jesuit priests brought sugar cane from Santo Domingo to Louisiana about 1751. It flourished in the rich soil of the Mississippi delta but for forty years was used only to make taffia, a variety of rum.

Antonio Mendez of St. Bernard Parish, Louisiana, succeeded in making sugar from the juice of the cane in 1791. Three years later Etienne de Bore planted great fields for the express purpose of producing sugar. His first crop brought him a net profit of about $12,000—then a very substantial sum. Before the end of the century it was apparent that the long period of independence upon bees for sweets was ended forever.

ICE CREAM

There is every reason to believe that the first ice cream was made without sugar and eggs and was an unexpected by-product of operations involving the use of ice to cool liquids. Well before the rebellious American colonists threw off the yoke of rule from overseas, some wealthy families were enjoying ice cream much like the modern product.

George Washington even purchased "a cream machine" that used ice. Proof of this transaction lies in the first President's detailed expense ledger, dated May 17, 1784.

That was just two years and one month before the first commerical venture into the manufacture and sale of ice cream. A Mr. Hall of New York City invested considerable capital in the first recorded ice cream company and advertised his wares for sale on June 8, 1786.

ICE-CREAM CONE

For more than a century after it was recognized as a commodity with a potential market, ice cream was dispensed in saucers and dishes. It seems never to have occurred to anyone that an edible pastry container for the ice cream would eliminate a lot of dishwashing—and add zest to the eating.

Much evidence supports the theory that the first ice cream cone was an impromptu device, fashioned during the 1904 Louisiana Purchase Exposition held in St. Louis. Traditions still current in the city that prides itself as being the "gateway to the West" say that an ice-cream seller exhausted his supply of dishes and spoons. In desperation he bought a supply of wafer-like pastries from a nearby vendor and tried selling the confection nestled in the top of a vaselike "cone." It was messy, but oh, so good!

Quickly improved and produced in quantity for the purpose of holding a scoop of cream, the ice-cream cone was being munched from coast to coast before the demolition of vacated Exposition buildings was completed.

CHOP SUEY

Though it is generally known that chop suey did not originate in China, few persons are aware that the dish is genuinely Chinese-American.

Li Hung-Chang, named ambassador to the United States by his emperor, created a sensation when he arrived in New York on August 28, 1896. His retinue included three cooks, five valets, his personal barber, and twenty-two household servants.

Greeted by President Grover Cleveland, he felt that his

nation's honor demanded that he make a grand gesture of some sort. He summoned his chefs and announced that he would give a dinner party the following evening. At it, he said, he wanted an entirely new dish served—one that would appeal to both Chinese and American guests.

Chop suey was the result of this order. From this beginning the popularity of the new dish spread across the United States and into China and other oriental countries—still prepared substantially as it was on August 29, 1896.

ROOT BEER

At a time when the Appalachian Mountains lay on the western frontier, colonists in North America became acquainted with an unusual native shrub. Roots of the sarsaparilla, they found, are rich in pungent compounds unlike anything found in the Old World. Dried and boiled, the roots yielded a syrup that was used in medicinal compounds such as homemade cough syrup.

In 1866 a student at the Jefferson Medical College, Philadelphia, became interested in the home remedy. He concluded that it was all but worthless for medicinal purposes, but he was intrigued by the novel flavor. Elmer Hires experimented for several months and finaly succeeded in preparing a tasty beverage flavored with sarsaparilla extract.

It came from the roots of the plant and looked a bit like some kinds of beer. Root beer, as Hires called his product, was first retailed in a Philadelphia drug store at five cents per mug. It made such a hit that its developer put other interests aside and 1876 started a national business making and selling the beverage.

MALTED MILK

Before the Civil War a few U.S. dairymen and housewives experimented with the drying of whole milk. No one was able to produce it in such fashion that it would keep.

William Horlick, of Racine, Wisconsin, decided that something should be added to powdered milk in order to preserve it. He tried numerous mixtures, finally hit upon the idea of combining dried whole milk with extract of wheat and malted barley. That was in 1882 or 1883.

Horlick's novel mixture not only kept; when pressed into tablets, persons ate it like candy. He called his concoction "Diastoid." Consumers soon dumped the sonorous name, though, and referred to the mixture that included milk and malted barley as "malted milk."

SUGAR CUBES

Henry Tate, reared in Lancashire, England, as the son of a Unitarian minister, got his start in business the hard way. He began as a grocer's assistant. He did not stay in that niche long, however. He first bought an interest in a store, then purchased it outright.

By the time he was forty the now prosperous businessman had turned his energies to one of the hottest commodities then being handled, sugar. To cut his cost of production he opened a refinery in London. It proved so successful that a second one was built.

About 1879, when he was sixty, Tate and his employees perfected a way to compress sugar into cubes that were easily handled, yet melted quickly. This discovery elevated him to top place in Europe's sugar industry.

With the fortune made from sugar cubes he purchased paintings by British artists and formed a discriminating collection made up of sixty-seven items carefully chosen by himself. In his old age he offered to give his art collection to the nation. Professional collectors and critics turned up their noses in disgust, wrote newspaper columns denouncing "a maker of sugar cubes who is seeking free publicity."

Today the Tate Gallery ranks with the best in the world and is visited by more than one million persons each year. Paintings chosen by the sugar-cube maker form the heart of the collection.

OYSTER COCKTAIL

Late in 1865 or early in 1866 a miner who had made a modest strike chose to celebrate in a California bar. He ordered a whisky cocktail plus a plate of select oysters—raw.

He downed his drink, then used the empty glass to douse his oysters with all the condiments in reach: Worcestershire sauce, catsup, and pepper sauce.

Those raw oysters went down to the accompaniment of loud expressions of delight. Seizing upon the idea, the bartender began offering all his patrons "oyster cocktails" for fifty cents a glass.

Documentary proof of the sequence of events is lacking, but traditions supporting it are so strong that experts in the history of gastronomy are inclined to regard it as substantially accurate.

POPCORN

Many persons regard popcorn as having been developed comparatively recently. Commercial sale of it in great volume did not begin until this century, but the tidbit itself is older than the United States. Indians who lived here long before the arrival of the first white men knew how to distinguish this queer grain from maize, as well as how to make it pop open.

English colonists first ate popcorn at the famous Thanksgiving dinner held on February 22, 1630. Quadequina, brother of Massasoit, was responsible. As his contribution to the big feast he brought deerskin bags that held several bushels of the special corn already "popped."

DOUGHNUT

The doughnut has been called "history's most delicious accident."

It was first made in the French hamlet of Montier-sur-Saulx late in 1917. Nearly one thousand U.S. soldiers stationed there developed the blues when days of heavy rain kept them endlessly soggy.

Two representatives of the Salvation Army, Brigadier Helen Parviance and Ensign Margaret Sheldon, set out to do something to boost morale. They mixed dough suitable for frying, rolled it with a milk bottle and used a tin milk can to cut round pieces from the dough. Fried on a crude brick stove that was open to wind and rain, the novel delicacy temporarily made men forget that they were wet and homesick.

No one knows who coined the name. It was all but inevitable, however. For the "doughboys" who wolfed them down admitted they were "nuts" to make such a commotion over bits of fried dough. Experiments soon proved that soggy middles could be eliminated by holes—and modern doughnuts were born.

BANANA

Until this century North Americans regarded the banana as a botanical curiosity rather than a source of food. A few trees of the many planted in botanical gardens yielded mature fruit, but no one in his right mind would have thought of eating a banana. Even in regions where the plant flourishes naturally, the banana tree was long utilized mainly as a source of shade for coffee shrubs.

Early attempts to whet American appetites for large red bananas failed; fruit of this sort does not ship well. Many workmen employed in building the Panama Canal became fond of the native yellow bananas—so prolific that a single stem sometimes bore as many as three hundred pieces of fruit.

Italian importers brought a few shiploads to New York and soon established a flourishing trade. By 1910, so many bananas entered New York annually that an enthusiastic eater of them calculated that "if placed end to end, in a single string, they would reach considerably more than twice around the earth."

BARBECUE

Late in the seventeenth or early in the eighteenth century, English-speaking adventurers visited Haiti. There they became acquainted with a native delicacy: meat of game animals roasted and smoked over an open fire. They probably mistook the name of the wooden framework on which the meat rested for the product it yielded. With its name clumsily adapted for the English-speaking world as "barbecue," it became a favorite in Georgia and other southeastern states.

Deer, wild boars, and other game animals were the mainstay of early barbecue lovers. As the supply of wild animals dwindled, it was natural to turn to domestic swine and oxen, and eventually to chickens.

Especially when a large carcass was cooked, no family could consume the meat before it spoiled. The barbecue became a frontier social event, gradually spreading north and west. Like the New England clambake, the community feast on roasted pork has diminished in importance but has not vanished. Meanwhile, restaurants specializing in barbecue have sprung up all over the United States and even overseas.

CANNED FOOD

Since the dawn of civilization, men have preserved various foods by processes such as drying and salting. Though sugar was scarce and costly until modern times, a few medieval kings even ate fruits and berries in winter—which their cooks had preserved by boiling them with generous quantities of sugar.

Late in the eighteenth century the French government offered a prize of twelve thousands francs to the person who would devise a means to "keep food over long periods of time, without use of substantial amounts of salt or sugar, yet wholly suitable for human consumption."

A Parisian confectioner, Nicholas Appert, collected the prize. By trial and error he found that many foods placed in containers and heated in boiling water before being sealed remained edible.

To the chagrin of French officials, Appert's method—though workable—didn't solve the pressing needs of military men. These required the development of a process by which thin sheets of iron were coated with a layer of tin to produce the modern "tin can." Use of glass containers, often with paraffin or a rubber seal or both, made the production of canned foods a household activity that, though once vital, is now fast disappearing under the impact of big commercial producers.

POTATO CHIPS

Even in many sections loyal to the Union food became quite scarce after the outbreak of the Civil War. Somewhere in the Washington-Philadelphia area, a Negro chef set out to give a little variety to the potatoes that were eaten every day. He cut them into thin pieces, or chips, and fried them—thus creating a dish that within a single century crossed practically all geographical and cultural boundaries.

Prepared exclusively in homes and restaurants for several decades, potato chips were first commercially manufactured in 1925 in Albany, New York.

MAPLE SUGAR

Under the influence of John Woolman and other zealots, the first general condemnations of slavery by an organized movement in the United States came from the Quakers. As a matter of conscience, many of them went beyond verbal condemnation. They flatly refused to buy, sell, or use any commodity in whose production slave labor was involved.

Sugar was high on the list of such items, for most of it came from the cane fields of the deep South.

As a substitute for the tainted product, many Quakers turned to maple syrup as a sweetening agent. Given impetus by this move, businessmen developed the now-thriving maple sugar industry.

KEY LIME PIE

Key lime pie wasn't planned. It just happened.

Sweetened condensed milk, first produced in quantity in 1857, was the main factor in development of the unique dessert.

Florida housewives were delighted to get milk of any kind after the hardships of war years. But many persons who used condensed milk objected to what they considered a "tinny" flavor. Those who didn't notice or didn't care about that factor often found condensed milk too sweet to suit them.

In an effort to cut the sweetness and kill the flavor that their husbands and children associated with exposure to tin, women on the Florida Keys squeezed local limes into canned milk. Just the right blend of condensed milk plus lime juice yielded a product that seemed ideal for making a pie filling in a hurry. When tested, it not only made the grade, but still remains popular even though the factors that produced it have dwindled into unimportance.

SUNDAE

The use of carbonated water to impart a fizz to soft drinks was a commercial success long before the general public lost a vaguely hostile attitude toward this concoction they did not quite understand. In many U.S. communities, laws regulating the Sabbath were amended to specify that no soda water should be dispensed on that day.

One or more drugstore owners managed to circumvent the local authorities by mixing fruits, nuts, and syrup with ice cream—but omitting the forbidden soda water. Tradition credits this maneuver to both Evanston, Illinois, and Norfolk, Virginia, Perhaps it was tried independently in both cities about the same time.

Consumers of the special "Sunday soda" quickly clipped the name of the dish to "sundae." It made such a hit that customers were soon asking for it on days when they could have had sodas without fear of the law.

PIE

Pastry-making began in Egypt, where the world's first full-time cooks were used in the kitchens of royal palaces. But even the finest of the cooks seem never to have stumbled on the idea of combining pastry with meat or fish.

This culinary advance took place in Greece, where the *artocreas* eventually became a staple. Made of hashed meat and bread, the dish—and the recipe for it—endured for centuries.

The first true pies made with two layers of crust and a thick layer of filling were baked by the Romans. Cato the Censor, a lover of delicacies, even preserved a recipe for a pie his countrymen called the *placenta*. Rye and wheat flour were mixed for the crust. Filled with honey plus cheese made from sheep's milk, this pie was rubbed with oil and then baked on bay leaves.

Fruit pies (or pasties) first appeared about 1600. Tradition credits Queen Elizabeth I with substituting preserved cherries for the usual meat or fish with which a pasty of the day was stuffed.

COFFEE

During the eighth or ninth century, inhabitants of some long lost village in the Near East experimented with seeds of a native plant. They may have been influenced by brush fires in which the wild plants were scorched. By chance or by design, they discovered that roasted seeds yield an enticing beverage when ground and boiled in water.

Shortly before the year A.D. 1000, coffee spread from the desolate interior of Ethiopia into surrounding regions. It crossed the Mediterranean and won many adherents in Europe before the time of the great Crusades.

For centuries Arabs made no precise distinction between wine and coffee but used *qahwah* as a label for both beverages. Today, fine Arabian coffee is highly prized by some gourmets —but the bulk of the world's annual production comes from South America.

BEVERAGE ALCOHOL

Under natural conditions a great many products ferment. Methods to control this natural process and to enhance the quality of liquid yielded by it were probably independently discovered dozens or even hundreds of times before the first crude methods of writing were devised.

References to alcohol are scattered throughout the very oldest of man's records, whether preserved in writing or transmitted by oral tradition. This holds true regardless of whether attention is focused on a great empire within the ancient cradle of civilization or a present-day aboriginal tribe.

There is no way to find convincing proof, but some noted students of human affairs believe that grain-bearing plants were first cultivated for the purpose of making beer.

With whatever ingredients that happened to be available, men have always managed to brew alcoholic beverages.

Ancient Mesopotamians—who had poor luck with grape orchards—made wine from dates and sesame seeds. Barley, rice, and other small grains have been used in many parts of the world. Maize, or Indian corn, was fermented by early inhabitants of the New World.

Launched in the dim mists of prehistory, the production and consumption of the intoxicant remains a major concern of Space Age man.

GERMAN CHOCOLATE CAKE

In spite of its name German chocolate cake did not originate in the land of the Rhine. Nor was it first concocted by a woman of German descent.

This popular modern delicacy gained more than local attention in 1957. That year a reader of the homemaking column of a Texas paper submitted a cake recipe that stipulated use of German's Sweet Chocolate—and no substitutes!

Picked up by columnists in other newspapers, the recipe was an instant winner. Homemakers a generation removed from the burst of national publicity accorded this triumph of the culinary art sometimes bake German chocolate cake—using a brand of chocolate other than the one that named the delicacy.

PIZZA

Though the date of his discovery is unknown, it was a commercial baker in Naples, Italy, who discovered that a dainty pie can be made without an upper crust. Perhaps he ran short of dough one day, sprinkled meat, cheese, and olives on top of a crust to avoid throwing a handful away.

Whatever the exact sequence of events may have been, it was soon found that a dish of this sort when baked was lip-smacking good. Very soon it became customary to use a pointed tool to cut indentations around the edge of the bread in order to make it look more attractive.

From Old Italian for "point," Neapolitans began to call the novel pie *pizza*. It spread to other Italian cities. Immigrants brought it with them to the United States, where it is now a naturalized citizen—universally accepted as a favorite American dish.

POOR BOY SANDWICH

In many European cities it has long been customary to slice small loaves of bread lengthwise. French nuns in old New Orleans continued this practice, but modified it by putting slices of cheese and meat between the pieces of bread.

A waif who knocked at the door of a convent and asked for a *pourboire*, or handout, never got cash. But the sisters always offered their visitor one of their special sandwiches.

With pronunciation of the French term *pourboire* slurred to sound like two English words, the "poor boy" was for decades almost as closely identified with New Orleans as was Bourbon Street. Visitors who sampled the unconventional sandwich liked it and took the idea home with them. Today, in almost any U.S. city, at least one restaurant is likely to serve sandwiches made like those formerly handed to waifs in the Mardi Gras city.

SPOON BREAD

Maize, or Indian corn, literally saved the lives of early European settlers in the New World. From it housewives learned to make mush (or porridge), thin hoecakes baked without leavening, and a variety of corn pones.

Spoon bread was created by accident. A Colonial house-wife whose name has not been preserved forgot to take the porridge off the fire one day. When she eventually remembered it—in consternation—and took the top off the earthen crock in which it had been simmering, she found that most of the water had evaporated.

Gingerly tested, because food of any kind was too precious to waste, it proved surprisingly good. Though a crust had formed over the top, the inside was creamy and tender.

There was just one way to serve it—with a large spoon.

This primitive type of spoon bread added variety to meals still dominated by various dishes made of corn. With eggs and milk added it became one of Virginia's most distinctive dishes.

PEPPER POT SOUP

During the siege of Valley Forge, morale among the troops dropped lower and lower as supplies of food dwindled in quality and quantity. A tradition dating from the era asserts that General Washington himself became concerned. He sent for one of his chief cooks, a Pennsylvania Dutchman, and insisted that "some tasty dish be prepared this very day."

The cook was eager to comply, but explained that he could not. He had absolutely nothing left except a few peppercorns given him by a village butcher.

"Use them!" Washington commanded.

That night weary, cold, and hungry men feasted on tripe heavily seasoned with peppercorns. They enjoyed the impro-vised dish so much that it became standard fare in the East and from that region spread throughout the United States.

ICED TEA

For decades after tea became an accepted beverage in Europe, Great Britain held a virtual monopoly on the com-modity. It became *the* nonalcoholic beverage of England, with teatime assuming as great importance as the modern coffee break.

Until 1904, everyone drank tea while it was quite hot. That year, Richard Blechynden (who was very, very British) visited the International Exposition in St. Louis. He set up a stall and tried to sell "dainty cups of the very best English tea" to Americans. The weather was so hot that no one was interested.

Faced with the prospect of going broke very quickly, the vendor was about ready to give up. One evening, at the time he usually prepared to close his stall, he dumped a quantity of crushed ice into a big urn of tea. Blechynden tasted it and to his astonishment found the new beverage delicious. He promptly switched to selling iced tea, recouped his losses, and launched a new food fashion.

Festivals and Holidays

ST. VALENTINE'S DAY

Ancient Romans placed great stress upon holidays that fell about the middle of the shortest month of the year. Dedicated to the goddess Juno, who was the wife of Jupiter, these festivals stressed love, courtship, and marriage.

That was appropriate since Juno, queen of heaven, was regarded as the special protector of women in "critical times of life."

Birds were usually mating in Italy by mid-February. Since all nature seemed to be preoccupied with the beginning of a new cycle of pairing off males and females, it was only natural that humans should do the same thing.

When Christianity became the official religion of the Roman Empire by edict of the Emperor Constantine, religious leaders immediately started trying to do away with pagan festivals. Many of them had been observed for so many centuries that they resisted all frontal attacks, so there were many efforts to bring about change in more subtle fashion. One of the most effective was substitution of a Christian observance for a pagan one, with special ceremonies held on or near the date of the long-established holiday.

Since the martyrdom of St. Valentine was celebrated on February 14, it made sense to stress homage to the man who was said to have been stoned to death on that day in A.D. 269. For that reason the name of a man about whom no written records exist came to be attached to the day formerly dedicated to Juno.

VALENTINE CARDS

The custom of valentines, or "giving Boys in writing the names of Girls to be admired and attended upon," was linked with February 14 long ago. St. Francis tried to do away with it by having names of saints written on slips of paper or "billets," and then drawn by both males and females.

Somehow the idea of getting the name of a saint by lottery and then paying special homage to that saint for the next twelve months did not quite supplant the much older custom of drawing names for sweethearts.

The exchange of printed greetings, sentimental or comic, is modern in origin. Samuel Pepys, author of one of the most famous diaries written in English, says the first Valentine illustrated with a drawing appeared on February 14, 1667. Other authorities dispute that date, and the chances of settling the argument with finality are dim.

Before the end of the seventeenth century, printers began producing limited numbers of cards with verses plus sketches. Postal rates were so high that most of these Valentines were delivered by hand.

Radical reduction in British postal rates fostered the practice of mailing Valentines. The fact that they could be sent anonymously probably led to the development of comic Valentines. Though no longer so popular as they were in the Victorian era, impudent or racy verses are still widely circulated about the middle of February.

45

"RING OUT THE OLD"

Until quite recent times Europeans used church bells to give signals and to make announcements. Skilled bell ringers used distinctive patterns of sounds to inform all within earshot that a citizen had died, that the town was being attacked by an enemy, or that a holiday had begun.

Bell ringing as an old year ended and a new one began was often complicated and almost frenzied. The custom originated as a way of making a special announcement by means of church bells; over a period of centuries the excitement of entering a new year led bell ringers to devise special "peals" for this occasion.

With bursts of sound from belfries long associated with the celebration late on New Year's Eve, the bells themselves were easily regarded as dynamic forces in the march of time. Once this notion became established, for bells to be rung at the turn of the year soon came to be regarded as essential; if they were not, the New Year might not come on time!

A Scandanavian variant of "ringing out the old, ringing in the new" involved ceremonial unbarring of house doors at midnight on the last day of the year. This was done so that the old year could be turned out of the house and the new year admitted.

EASTER, FESTIVAL OF THE MOON

Since printed calendars identifying Easter have become commonplace, awareness of the holy day's link with the moon has dimmed—this in spite of general recognition that the date on which it falls can vary from March 22 to April 25. However, the moon accounts for this queer fluctuation in date.

Many early Christians celebrated Easter at Passover, whose date is determined by the moon rather than the sun. Hostility against Jews and Jewish customs led to formal debates in councils of the Church.

At the Council of Nicea in A.D. 325, an extraordinarily complicated set of rules was adopted. Henceforth, said churchmen,

Easter must be observed "on the first Sunday after the first full moon on or after the spring equinox [March 21st]."

Only an expert can determine the date of Easter according to that formula. Even the experts goofed in 1818, when Easter was observed on the wrong day. Anti-Jewish sentiment to the contrary, Easter occasionally falls on the fourteenth day of Nisan, the holiday that Fathers of the Church were trying to avoid.

Rooted in ancient veneration for the moon, the date of Easter was long regarded as symbolizing the rebirth of living things that had passed through the death of winter. Eostre, the Anglo-Saxon goddess who presided over the vernal equinox, eventually gave her name to the Christian festival.

EGG ROLLING

The rolling of eggs at Easter has its roots in antiquity. For centuries, pious farmers rolled eggs across their fields at this season in order to make sure that the ground would be fertile.

The modern game of hunting eggs hidden by parents is a survival from this semimagical practice. Though the term "rolling" is still attached to some celebrations—especially those that attract large numbers of participants—the custom of actually rolling eggs over the earth has long since disappeared.

HOT CROSS BUNS

Eating special buns at the festival of the pagan goddess Eostre has long been an established custom among the natives of Britian. Early Christian missionaries who tried to stop this practice got nowhere.

Eventually a compromise was reached. Converts to the religion in which the cross is the central symbol were permitted to continue eating buns at the time of the spring festival—but only if the tidbits were marked with the sign of the cross.

Once hot cross buns became standard fare at Easter, many bakers worked hard so that patrons could get them directly from the oven. Served piping hot with a crude cross of sugar on top, an Easter bun was thought to bring good luck. Though most of the bun's power to bring good luck vanished after it became cold, one specimen of the baker's art was customarily saved since it was considered proper to use crumbs from it as a household remedy during the months that followed Easter.

THE EASTER PARADE

The departure of winter, which is linked with the spring equinox, is significant even in sunny Mediterranean lands. It is all-important in Britain, Scandanavia, Germany, and other parts of northern Europe.

Especially in these northern regions, it was customary to put on a new article of clothing to celebrate the beginning of the new cycle of warmth, planting, growth, and harvest.

Today's Easter parade is simply a more lavish and more elaborate version of the Old World rites in which every villager tried to have a new hat or a new pair of shoes or at least a new kerchief to wear for worship, egg rolling, and other festivities linked with the coming of spring.

EASTER EGGS

Whether genuine or artificial, Easter eggs are symbolic reminders of the new life that is wrapped up in an egg and brought to Earth each spring with "the return of the sun" when days begin to grow longer.

Long before the Christian festival of Easter was established, persons of many cultures exchanged eggs at the time of the year when nature wakes up from sleep. Wealthy persons used to cover their gift eggs with gilt or even gold leaf; ordinary persons usually colored them red.

Today's egg hunt, involving a dozen or hundreds or thousands of decorated or candy eggs, is so gay that it conceals the reverence with which many ancients regarded this symbol of "life out of death."

Both Greeks and Romans buried eggs—sometimes real, sometimes fashioned from gold, silver, or semiprecious stones—in the tombs of the wealthy and great. Most archaeologists consider this practice an indication that these people believed in immortality, or life after death, even before being exposed to Christian influences.

CHRISTMAS CARDS

In the United States alone, an estimated two billion greeting cards are mailed during the Christmas season each year.

This most popular of all seasonal greetings has zoomed to the top in a bit more than a century—after getting off to a very slow start.

Along with half a dozen other claimants, London artist Joseph Cundall credited himself with publishing the first Christmas card in 1846. Less than a thousand copies of Cundall's card were sold.

By the middle of the 1850's Christmas cards—in the form of engraved wishes for "A Merry Christmas" on slips about the size of visiting cards—were more common.

Prussian lithographer-artist Louis Prang introduced Christmas cards into the United States. His first designs, which were printed in Europe, went on sale in Boston in 1874. The cards caught the fancy of the public, attracted a host of imitators, and have been increasing in popularity ever since.

CHRISTMAS TREES

Many countries claim the distinction of having launched the custom of erecting Christmas trees, but it may have begun independently in several parts of Europe. Ceremonial worship of trees in ancient pagan rites almost certainly led to the decoration of trees at the time of the winter solstice.

German emigrants brought with them the custom of setting up trees in their houses at Christmas. Partly because it was a colorful practice, partly because trees were to be had for the cutting, the custom spread rapidly through all segments of U.S. society.

MISTLETOE

Sprigs of mistletoe garnered from forest giants can't be mass produced, so only plastic varieties are universally available for Christmas decoration. The limited supply of the real thing brings good prices, though, for everyone knows that a few mistletoe leaves and berries used during the holidays will foster good luck during the coming year.

Why mistletoe instead of some other plant? Because this parasite which draws its nurture from oaks and other trees was regarded by the Druids of ancient Britain as endowed with supernatural power. One of their legends credits the mistle thrush, who was a messenger of the gods, with having brought the plant to earth.

Druids used mistletoe as a cure for sickness, a shield against the power of witches, and as a potent source of good luck. A kiss given under a sprig of the mysterious plant was interpreted to be a promise of marriage.

Christians tried for centuries to discourage any use of mistletoe at any season of the year. The deeply ingrained practices rooted in festivals observed around the time of the modern Christmas proved too stubborn to be eliminated, however. As a result, the plant that has no visible link with the ground and is totally dependent upon the trees where it takes root gradually won acceptance as one of the things especially desired at Christmas.

DECEMBER 25

Neither scripture nor secular history records the date of Jesus' birth; even the season of the year is not stipulated. Some evidence points to spring, but it is not conclusive. The only thing reasonably certain about the coming of the Christ Child is that his birth did not take place in winter.

The festival of "Christes Masse" (or Christ's birth) was celebrated very early—at a variety of times and seasons. In A.D. 350 Pope Julius I formally designated December 25 as Christmas.

He chose that date because it coincided with important pagan festivals. These, in turn, were linked with the winter solstice (usually December 22) when day and night are exactly the same length.

The ancients, who were far more conscious of the movements of heavenly bodies than are most persons of modern times, had astonishingly accurate knowledge of astronomy. In the period before the winter solstice the sun seems to die a bit every day, for in the northern hemisphere the interval between sunrise and sunset is reduced daily. All this changes after the day on which sunlight and darkness are exactly equal. Gradually lengthening days herald the rebirth of the sun and call for a celebration.

Veneration for the life-giving rays of the all-important sun, coupled with precise knowledge about the annual cycle of dwindling and then lengthening days, established December 25 as the logical date for one of the most important of all festivals.

CHRISTMAS STOCKINGS

Stockings hung by the fireplace with care at Christmas time are a living tribute to the influence of a poem.

" 'Twas the Night Before Christmas" was written by Clem-

51

ent C. Moore who thought it would injure his reputation as a scholar if he signed his name to it. After it was published anonymously in 1823, the poem created such a stir that he admitted authorship.

Receptacles in which St. Nicholas could place gifts for good children had been used much earlier. In Holland, children put their wooden shoes in chimney corners on Christmas Eve. Stockings were used by some Americans during the eighteenth century but not by all.

Magnified by its prominent role in the most famous of all Christmas poems, the stocking has become a permanent feature of North American celebrations.

MANGER SCENES

Manger scenes have been used for centuries. Some towns and cities go to great trouble and expense to be sure their displays are just right.

A person need make only the most superficial check of the accounts of the first Christmas in order to discover that there are no details about the number and kinds of creatures who gathered about the manger.

Inevitably, national differences in manger scenes developed, since the animals with which children are familiar vary from one land to another. The use of camels in modern American manger scenes is colorful but has no scriptural basis, as no gospel writer gives even a hint about the kind of animals used by the Wise Men.

"DECK THE HALLS WITH BOUGHS OF HOLLY"

The Druids of prehistoric Britain revered the plant we know as the holly. To them its evergreen leaves constituted proof positive that the sun never deserted it. Consequently, they used the plant as medicine, as a protective device to ward off evil spirits, and even as a good luck charm against lightning. Their celebration of the New Year coincided closely with the season that the Church later designated as a holy period in honor of Jesus' birth. It was all but inevitable that the use of the semisacred plant should become linked with the Christian celebration that supplanted the older pagan one. Many scholars even think that "holly" is an adaptation of an early form of the word *holy*.

The use of the holly and its associations with Christmas were not limited to Britain, however. In Germany the prickly plant was widely called *Christ-thorn* because the prickly points of the leaves were regarded as reminders that Jesus wore a crown of thorns. To complete the symbolism, the brilliant red berries of the plant were treated as symbolic of the drops of blood Jesus shed.

Honored in both secular and religious verse, holly is so closely associated with Christmas that it has been adopted for decorative use during the holiday season even in regions where it cannot be grown.

CHRISTMAS CAROLS

Throughout the Middle Ages villagers in many parts of Europe, notably France, participated in various "ring dances" that were held in the streets. A ring dance is somewhat like a game of Ring-Around-the-Rosy accompanied by song. Melodies used in ring dances are believed to have inspired the first songs of joy used in honor of the nativity.

For centuries small bands of persons roamed the streets at Christmastime and stopped at intervals to sing carols. Both words and melodies were transmitted orally.

No collection of printed Christmas carols was issued prior to the early-sixteenth century; even then, copies were scarce and costly.

Puritans made a valiant but unsuccessful effort to suppress carol-singing, which they considered a concession to pagan tastes. The practice, which is at least eight centuries old, is losing some of its hold in urban centers. But even in our biggest cities groups of children and youth often sing under the windows of friends, notables, and invalids.

POINSETTIA

Adoption of the poinsettia as *the* Christmas flower is recent and Western in origin.

Native to Mexico where it is often called "flower of the blessed night," the plant whose crimson leaves add just the right touch of color to many a decorative scheme is highly sensitive to light. Its leaves turn red in response to intervals of light and darkness of a certain length. In its native habitat those intervals occur so that the plant is at its best during the Christmas season.

Joel Poinsett of South Carolina, onetime diplomat who served in Mexico, was intrigued by the flower that often became bright during the "blessed night" on which the Savior's birth is commemorated. He brought the plant to this country, where it took his name but remained rare and exotic until recent generations.

Now florists have learned how to control the plant's development in such fashion that practically all poinsettias are at their brilliant best when Christmas is celebrated in North America. Air freight has made it possible to use poinsettias all over the world. As a result, the popularity of the only Christmas plant that is native to the New World has spread to every continent.

Invention and Discovery

LIFEBOAT

During periods when winds were high and water was rough, sailing vessels sometimes sank within English harbors. Townsfolk would gather to watch; sometimes they saw sailors drop from the rigging one by one and drown. There was no way to help, for any boat in existence would quickly sink in so rough a sea.

Lionel Lukin, a coachbuilder who worked in the Long Acre section of London, set out to build an "unsubmergible boat" that could be used for rescue purposes.

He first exhibited a model about 1784. Encouraged by the Prince of Wales (later King George IV), the landlubber created a boat with a hollow, watertight compartment. As additional insurance against sinking, he added a projecting gunwale of cork to the upper frame.

Lukin's lifeboat, which had a straight keel, was soon modified by substitution of a curved keel. Today the basic concept of the carriage-builder—that of an unsinkable boat—is used in lifeboats and pleasure craft the world around. Lukin's tombstone bears this inscription:

This Lionel Lukin
was the first who built a life-boat, and was the original inventor
of that principle of safety by which many lives
and much property have been preserved from shipwreck,
and he obtained for it the King's Patent
in the year 1785

PENDULUM CLOCK

On a holy day in 1581 the Cathedral of Pisa was crowded with worshipers. One of them, a boy of seventeen, forgot his prayers as he watched a lamp. Pulled aside for lighting, it swung first in wide arcs, then in shorter and shorter ones. Unbelievable though the idea was, it seemed to the boy that it took the lamp as long to complete a short arc as a wide one. Having no other way to time the lamp's movements, he used his own pulse to check against and found that a long movement took no more pulsebeats than a short one.

Galileo Galilei spent his life probing the secrets of masses in motion, the science of dynamics. He designed military machines, taught physics at the University of Padua, and invented the telescope; but he never forgot that swinging lamp.

Late in life, and already blind, he conceived the idea of applying such a motion to a mechanical timekeeping device. He died a year later and his son proved incapable of completing the instrument suggested by his father.

Dutch physicist Christian Huygens attacked the problem. He designed and executed a pendulum-escapement device and described it to the world in 1656. The pendulum clock, activated by a motion whose mysteries were dimly glimpsed by a boy at worship, paved the way for the industrial revolution.

FERRIS WHEEL

George Washington Gale Ferris, a native of Galesburg, Illinois, studied mechanical engineering at Rensselaer Polytechnic Institute. Soon after his graduation in 1881 he was sent to supervise the erection of what was then one of the world's great bridges, the railroad bridge spanning the Ohio River at Henderson, Kentucky.

This job was completed during a period of national excitement over the impending World's Columbian Exposition at Chicago.

Ferris conceived the idea of building a gaint revolving wheel and sold Exposition officials on it. He made parts in Pittsburgh, shipped them to Chicago, and there assembled a "wheel" that carried 1,440 passengers. It was 250 feet in diameter, 790 feet in circumference, and weighed 1,070 tons. A prime attraction of the Columbian Exposition, it was regarded as one of the mechanical wonders of the world.

Profitable operation of such a monster required huge crowds. The wheel was moved to St. Louis for the Exposition of 1904, and was eventually dismantled and sold as scrap—for just $1,800.

Miniature versions of Ferris' great wheel, scaled down to heights ranging from 40 to 55 feet and designed to carry twenty-four to thirty-two passengers, became a hit at amusement parks and fairs. A Ferris Wheel 300 feet in diameter, built in 1897 for a London Exhibition, is the biggest one still in use.

Ferris himself died at age thirty-seven without ever having patented his invention.

SAFETY RAZOR

Men have been scraping whiskers off their faces since the earliest artisans learned how to make metal blades. During many centuries, all makers of razors have tried to produce blades that would last as long as possible.

King C. Gillette of Brookline, Massachusetts, made his living as a bottle cap salesman. Perhaps because he dealt with a product with a short life-expectancy, he deliberately set about inventing something—anything—that would be used in quantity and then thrown away.

Gillette considered and then discarded one idea after another. One morning as he shaved he found his razor so dull that he knew he'd have to take it to a professional for sharpening. In a flash of insight he conceived the idea of making thin blades at low cost, to be discarded after a few uses.

It took the salesman several years to develop his radical new razor and to find financial backing for small-scale manufacture. His razor appeared on the market in 1903; within fifteen years more than three hundred competitors were bidding for customers.

Gillette's breakthrough not only made the safety razor practical (in contrast to earlier ones whose blades required honing), but also launched the technological explosion in throw-away merchandise that has led to everything from paper "bottles" for milk to one-wear dresses.

SEWING MACHINE

Lame from birth, Elias Howe wasn't strong enough to do farm work. So he became an apprentice in a machine shop that specialized in repairing precision instruments. As a result of a chance remark by a customer, he decided to give up his job and invent a sewing machine.

He mastered most of the problems, but no machine he built would sew a straight seam or produce regular stitches.

One evening in 1844 he went to bed tired from working all day at the job of producing half a dozen more needles—made like all those that had "worked," with eyes in the center. Howe dreamed that he was in a far-off land. Primitive warriors captured him and brought him before their king, who gave him twenty-four hours to produce a sewing machine or face the death penalty.

In his frenzied dream he worked feverishly without success. At the end of his day of grace, hordes of savages surrounded him to escort him to the place of execution. Each warrior brandished a spear. But the spears were not ordinary ones; each had a hole near its point.

Waking from his vivid dream, the self-taught inventor knew he had his answer. He shifted the hole in his needle from the center to the point, and the sewing machine became a reality.

ELECTRIC MOTOR

Michael Faraday, who had little formal schooling, learned the trade of bookbinder. While working at it he applied to the great Sir Humphrey Davy for a job and was employed as a handyman. Through constant but informal contact with the scientist, Faraday learned enough about electricity to serve as an expert witness in cases involving the strange new force.

During a ten-year period that began in 1821, Faraday gave most of his time and attention to original experiments in electricity. It was already known that electricity can create magnetic fields; Faraday reasoned, as a consequence, that magnetic fields should have power to generate electric current.

Any expert could have told him it was impossible. But since his education had stopped at age thirteen, Faraday did not know it couldn't be done.

Most of Faraday's efforts failed. On August 29, 1831, he wound some wire around one segment of a six-inch, soft iron ring and attached the coil to a battery. Another coil halfway around the ring was linked with a galvanometer. According to this amateur's reasoning, current flowing through the first coil should induce a flow of electricity in the second by means of magnetic influences. Incredibly, the device worked. For the first time in history, mechanical energy had been converted into electricity. Faraday's discovery gave the world all the essentials of the electric motor, dynamo, and transformer.

PRINTING PRESS

Johann Gensfleisch was born in Mainz, Germany, between 1394 and 1399. As an adult he dropped his father's name and took his mother's, a decision that made the name Gutenberg famous around the world.

Early in the 1440's Gutenberg abandoned the family trade of goldsmith and began experimenting with printing. Already familiar with coin-stamping and wax seals, he learned how to make and use wood engravings. He dreamed of printing with movable type, but the clumsy hand processes used by printers of the era were not suitable for development of the idea.

One autumn afternoon Gutenberg helped with the wine harvest. Though he had seen similar machines many times before, he looked at the powerful winepress with new eyes. "I watched the wine flowing," he later recalled, "and going back from the effect to the cause, I studied the power of this press which nothing can resist."

Slightly modified, the instrument that had been designed to squeeze the juice from grapes became a working printing press, sufficiently powerful to yield good, clear impressions even though the metal segments bearing individual letters weren't absolutely uniform in length.

TYPEWRITER

William Austin Burt very much wanted a voice in government. He conducted a vigorous campaign and was elected to the Michigan Territorial Legislative Council in 1826. Almost immediately he found himself deluged with paper work.

Burt, who already had a reputation for being extremely clever with his hands, borrowed an assortment of type from the *Michigan Gazette*. He fastened individual letters to a wheel, then designed a lever so that when the wheel rotated a chosen letter could be pressed against the paper. Patented in 1829, the device won its inventor the title of "typographer."

Built chiefly of wood, the heavy boxlike machine backfired— it took legislator Burt longer to write with it than by hand. Later inventors abandoned the principles used in the first writing machine that was designed specifically as a time-saver and began placing letters on individual, finger-operated keys.

Now the wheel has come full circle. Using electricity in lieu of slow hand-movements, typists around the world are employing, more and more, machines on which letters on a circular type segment spin rapidly from one position to another in order to achieve the speed lacking in Burt's pioneer device.

GAS MASK

Germany declared war on France early in August, 1914. Both armies dug in for a long artillery duel, and there were relatively few actual movements of troops during the fall and winter.

In April, 1915, German troops began a strong movement to capture the port of Calais on the English Channel. As a surprise maneuver, they made the first battlefield use of poison gas. Chlorine caused the French to choke and weep and enabled their foes to gain nearly three miles. Then the supply of gas was exhausted; French reinforcements arrived, and Calais was not again threatened until 1918.

During the weeks that the Germans waited to manufacture more gas, French physiologist André Mayer and a British colleague, John Barcroft, were hard at work. Their gas mask—forerunner of all modern ones—was conceived, designed, and manufactured in a period of about three weeks. By the time their foes returned with new supplies of chlorine, the Allies had enough gas masks to allow them to remain in their trenches and withstand the next attack.

LINOTYPE

"Composition," or the process of setting type by hand, was almost unbelievably slow and tedious. The cost of printing using this method was so great that at the time of the American Revolution, less than one hundred libraries in the New World held as many as three hundred books.

In the 1820's inventors began a frenzied race to perfect a machine that would do the work of trained fingers. At least one hundred "composing machines" were patented; though some cost their developers more than one million dollars, none proved workable.

A court stenographer who wanted a way to speed up his work met a twenty-two-year-old German instrument maker in 1876. James O. Clephane suggested to Ottmar Mergenthaler that a mechanical device to set type would bring him easy money very quickly.

Mergenthaler, who knew nothing whatever about printing, set to work. After ten years of frustration he produced a highly complicated machine. Each of its ninety keys controlled a tube filled with molds, or matrices, for a letter or symbol. When the keys were pressed, matrices were released into a line the width of a newspaper column; then molten metal flowed into a slot underneath and a solid line of type was ejected.

Demonstrated in the office of the *New York Tribune* on July 3, 1886, the Linotype revolutionized printing. At the time it was perfected daily newspapers in the United States had a combined circulation of about four million copies. Within twenty years after Mergenthaler's mechanical marvel went on sale, their circulation had climbed to more than thirty million.

COTTON GIN

Yale graduate Eli Whitney knew nothing about life in the South until he was invited to be a guest of Mrs. Nathanael Greene at her plantation in Georgia. During the winter of 1792–93 the Massachusetts native discovered at first hand the extent to which cotton dominated the lives of plantation folk.

Picking cotton in the fields was a slow and laborious job, but the task of removing the fibers from the seeds was even worse. In almost casual fashion Mrs. Greene suggested that her guest from up north should invent a machine to perform the job of separating lint from seeds.

Whitney conceived and discarded a variety of ideas. Strolling in the moonlight one evening he saw a cat trying to pull a chicken from a coop. The space between the slats was too narrow for the fowl's body, so each time the cat withdrew its paw it held nothing except a mass of feathers.

An iron claw that would draw cotton fibers through narrow openings too small for seeds, Whitney reasoned, should do the job suggested by his hostess. Within a week Eli Whitney had worked out the first crude diagram of his proposed cotton gin; he patented it in 1794 and began manufacturing his machine in partnership with the manager of Mrs. Greene's plantation.

SYNTHETIC DYESTUFFS

A. W. von Hoffmann, of the best-known German chemists of the 1840's, had a dream. One day, he said, someone would produce synthetic quinine. By means of it the laboratory would free man of dependence upon nature in his never-ending struggle to get enough medicine with which to treat malaria.

Most persons who heard Hofmann talk of synthetic quinine shrugged off the idea as an impossible dream. But one of the chemist's assistants, William Henry Perkin, took the idea seriously.

Perkin knew that the chemical formula of quinine is $C_{20}H_{24}N_2O_2$. He took it for granted that the medical substance would be formed if the right number of the right atoms could be made to combine. (Neither he nor any of his contemporaries guessed that an immense number of possible combinations of the same atoms could form a great variety of substances.)

Working during the Easter vacation of 1856 Perkin started with a derivative of coal (rich in carbon). He didn't get anything close to quinine—but he did produce a salt that proved to be rich in coloring matter. Aniline purple, or "mauveine," was the first synthetic dye. It laid the foundation for an immense chemical industry and rekindled enthusiasm for research into the nature of man-made substances.

At the time he made his monumental discovery, Perkin was just eighteen years old.

X RAYS

Wilhelm Conrad Roentgen spent much of his life investigating problems of pure physics. As a professor at Würzburg, Germany, he had considerable time but only the most primitive equipment.

Earlier it had been found that some evacuated tubes emit cathode rays. No one knew what to make of this phenomenon. So Roentgen set out to investigate it. Using a Crookes tube to produce the radiation he wished to study, he shielded the apparatus with black cardboard that he knew to be opaque to all forms of light.

One day in November, 1895, he found that a screen of a barium compound placed near the experimental table became fluorescent after current had flowed through the tube. Other investigators had noticed similar phenomena but paid them little heed.

Roentgen reasoned that in addition to cathode rays, his tube was emitting some other form of radiation with previously unheard-of powers of penetration. Since he hadn't the foggiest notion of its nature, he called the unknown phenomenon the X ray. Within two months, on January 20, 1896, doctors Oudin and Bathélemy made the first X-ray photograph of human bone structure, a fuzzy but indisputable picture of bones of the hand made through their subject's flesh.

NYLON

Wallace H. Carothers and a team of organic chemists at E. I. du Pont de Nemours and Co. were intrigued by a riddle of nature. They wanted to know why certain kinds of small molecules have the capacity to combine with one another and form giant molecules.

Working with the technical problem of polymerization, they used a variety of raw materials. One day a scientist tried to remove a sample of molten polymer from a vessel. He became annoyed when the sticky stuff yielded a tangle of long, elastic fibers or "threads."

Carothers seized on the unexpected property of polymers, and led in the development of their potential uses. He squirted some of the strange stuff from a hypodermic needle, found that a strong and uniform fiber was formed.

It was an easy step from hypodermic needle to a spinnerette designed to extrude molten polymer at a specific rate. The material produced by it was nylon—first of the synthetic fibers, which have come from the laboratory rather than from plants and animals.

AIR BRAKE

George Westinghouse was perpetually in a hurry. He was so eager to grow up that he ran away from home at age fifteen and joined the army. At his father's insistence he later tried college. Campus life proved too dull for him, though, and he gave up his studies after one year.

Riding a passenger train one day in 1866, when he was twenty, he was delayed by an accident. Railroaders explained that it took a long time to stop a train. Each car was equipped with an individual set of handwheels operated by brakemen.

While he waited for the tracks to be cleared, Westinghouse decided he'd find a way to enable engineers to apply brakes to all the wheels of a train simultaneously. Oldtimers laughed in his face when he suggested the ridiculous idea.

He persisted, though, and experimented with steam. While testing his apparatus he read a magazine article about use of compressed air for activating drills in construction of a Swiss tunnel. As soon as he read the article, he knew he had the key to his invention.

At twenty-three, Westinghouse formed his Air Brake Company—with capitalization of $500,000. He tried to see Commodore Vanderbilt in order to get his support, but the financier sent him word, "I have no time to waste upon fools."

The air brake, with its basic principles unchanged, is still in use around the world as the most feasible way of stopping trains rapidly to avoid collisions that might annoy travelers—travelers less creative than the young man in a hurry.

PNEUMATIC TIRE

Scottish veterinarian John Dunlop threatened to take away his son's tricycle if the boy didn't stop falling and hurting himself. Warnings had no effect, since the child had no place to ride except the rough cobblestone streets of Belfast. Nothing could be done about the streets, his father recognized. So any change would have to come as a result of an improvement in the vehicle.

John Dunlop devised a way to fill rubber tubes with compressed air, then placed one on each wheel of his son's tricycle.

This pneumatic tire proved so effective that a prominent bicycle racer borrowed the idea. Most folk of the era joked about "riding on air," but a few idealists ventured to suggest that the concept could even be applied to carriages.

In 1888, the air-filled "bolster" tire was adopted by numerous bicycle racers in spite of the fact that most experts thought the device to be ridiculous. Successfully tried on carriages, it was later adapted to the horseless carriage by French pioneers in the auto industry.

CELLULOID

The growing shortage of ivory from elephants plus the popularity of billiards created the climate that led to discovery of celluloid, man's first plastic.

A manufacturer of billiard balls sponsored a competition for an ivory substitute. Most persons who entered the contest used natural substances. John Wesley Hyatt, a young printer in Albany, New York, attacked the problem in a different way. Pyroxylin, then entering general use as an ingredient in lacquers and coating materials, seemed to offer promise—if it could be made permanently hard.

Hyatt mixed pyroxylin (produced by treating cotton with nitric acid) with solid camphor and produced a fine ivory-like substance. Celluloid never quite made the grade as a substitute for ivory on the billiard table. But the grandfather of all present-day plastics proved just right for making wipe-clean collars, cuffs, and even shirt fronts. Adapted for the manufacture of combs, denture plates, shoe horns, and other common household objects, celluloid launched what eventually became one of the first billion-dollar industries in the United States.

CELLULOID FILM

The Rev. Hannibal W. Goodwin, a Protestant Episcopal clergyman, wasn't satisfied with the quality of the photographs he took. Some basic changes were needed, he insisted, and the then new substance called celluloid offered great promise for use in making film.

In spite of the snickers of his parishioners the priest continued with his experiments until he learned how to make celluloid strips of practically unlimited length. He applied for a patent on May 2, 1887.

George Eastman, who is alleged to have had a clerk in the U.S. Patent Office on his own payroll, had pioneered in industrial espionage. Tipped off by his informant, Eastman changed the radical new idea slightly and rushed through his own patent.

After extensive litigation the clergyman received his patent on September 13, 1898, and collected millions of dollars in damages from Eastman. Though highly inflammable and subject to becoming brittle with age, the celluloid strips developed by the Rev. Goodwin were used in practically all early movies.

MOTION PICTURES

Leland Stanford, a horse lover wealthy enough to indulge in expensive whims, set out about 1850 to prove that when a horse runs he sometimes has all four feet off the ground simultaneously. Stanford bought twelve cameras (equipped with the glass plates then in use) and set them up at intervals along a racetrack.

Photographers of the day found they couldn't make shots fast enough to get a series of connected pictures. A young railroad engineer, John D. Isaacs, devised a system of electric wires and connected them with cameras. He managed to get a coordinated series of photos (one of which showed the running animal with all four feet off the ground) that set the stage for the development of motion pictures.

Strips of celluloid film replaced glass; George Eastman perfected "roller photography" and Thomas Edison and many other great inventors added refinements to the making and projecting of pictures. Even the most sophisticated present-day movie consists, however, of a series of coordinated photos taken in rapid succession—and exposed so briefly to viewers that the human eye fails to notice the break between one picture and the next.

COLT REVOLVER

Sam Colt had no financial pressures; he just didn't like school. That's why he quit at age ten and took a job in his father's factory.

Soon the novelty of tending the machines that made silk and woolen goods wore off. Sam began spending more and more of his time with other idle boys. In desperation his father shipped him off to school in Amherst, Massachusetts. That was in 1828.

Amherst didn't hold Sam Colt long. He ran away, misrepresented his age, and managed to sign on as a member of the crew of a merchant ship engaged in transporting goods between America and India.

Already an expert with a Yankee jackknife, he spent much of his free time whittling. On the return voyage he admitted to fellow sailors that he wasn't exactly wasting his time but was making a model of a brand new kind of firearm.

Veteran tars laughed at the sixteen-year-old and his pretensions. Even when he had completed a rather fancy-looking wooden weapon, his shipmates persisted in calling him "Whittler."

But it was from that model carved during the lonely months of the voyage from Calcutta to Boston that the Colt revolver was made. One of the most influential firearms of all time, it has been described as "the gun that won the West."

"SINGING PLOW"

Very early in their penetration of the vast North American continent, settlers recognized that the types of plows that had been used for centuries in Europe were not suitable for the New World. Thomas Jefferson studied the problem and correctly concluded that the implement must have a cutting edge that would produce a straight furrow.

Attempts to make such a plow from wood proved futile. So the first patented plow of cast iron was developed in 1793. It performed satisfactorily under some conditions but most farmers refused to use it for fear it would poison the ground.

The sticky soil of the Midwest clung to cast-iron plows almost as tenaciously as to wooden ones. Many experimental designs were tried, but none of them worked.

In 1833 a youthful metalworker from Illinois, John Deere, leaped to the conclusion that the problem lay in the metal itself rather than its shape. Using a discarded circular saw from a sawmill, Deere fashioned the world's first steel plow. Because implements equipped with it vibrated as they moved steadily through all kinds of soil, Deere's plow was called the "singing plow" and soon replaced all earlier ones. Along with rapid-fire weapons and barbed wire, this plow made possible the conquest of the western frontier.

BARBED WIRE

U.S. cattle raisers who pushed into the Great Plains states before the Civil War found plenty of grass. The lack of timber created a problem they hadn't faced back east, however. It was difficult and costly to build fences in the West.

Numerous ranchers bought rolls of number nine round or oval wire and tried stringing a single strand of the heavy stuff from post to post. Cattle liked to rub against such fences and broke them with exasperating frequency.

During the 1860's, at least three inventors secured patents for wire equipped with spikes to deter cattle from pushing down fences. None of these inventions were successful.

Joseph F. Glidden of DeKalb, Illinois, decided to approach the problem from a different perspective. He cut barbs from sheet metal, inserted them between two light wires, and twisted the wires. Patent number 157 124, granted on November 1, 1873, to a man who had never been close to a big cattle farm, brought Glidden's heirs a fortune and revolutionized the manufacture of wire.

TRAFFIC LIGHT

Detroit, Michigan, was the first city in the world to have such heavy automobile traffic that vehicles sometimes became snarled at intersections. Something ought to be done about it, reasoned Officer William L. Potts of the city police department. Why use men to do poorly a job that could be done more efficiently with electricity?

Potts worked out an electric light system to regulate the flow of cars, buggies, and wagons. For the colors he borrowed from the practice of railroaders, who had long been accustomed to the use of green for "go," red for "stop," and amber for "caution."

The policeman's system, when installed in a tower, permitted him to control three intersections instead of one. In 1920, the year they were first used, the newfangled traffic lights were the talk of the town. Several inventors later challenged the priority of Potts's development, but a U.S. District Court, after hearing lengthy testimony, ruled in favor of the man who had put his brain to work because his feet were tired.

TRANSISTOR

In preparation for the coming holidays three Bell Telephone laboratory scientists worked late on December 23, 1947. Methodically testing electrical properties of one substance after another, they turned their attention to the little-known element *germanium.*

To their surprise, when a small piece of the obscure substance was used, a speech signal was amplified about forty times. Their report of Case No. 38139-7, dated the day before Christmas, 1947, is still preserved. It includes a sketch of the circuit used and points out that germanium gave a distinct gain in speech level with no noticeable change in quality.

The applications of this to the communications industry were obvious and immediate. Not so obvious was the fact that the "transistor effect," as it came to be called, would lead to miniaturization of electronic equipment—and from that to the modern computer. For having instantly recognized the potential importance of the phenomenon they had found as they rushed to clean up their work before the holidays, John Bardeen, Walter Brattain, and William Shockley received the 1956 Nobel Prize.

71

CHRISTMAS TREE LIGHTS

Until 1917, candles were in universal use to light Christmas trees. There were many fires, but no one knew how to eliminate the hazard of open flames on inflammable trees.

A family of Spanish immigrants to the United States specialized in the manufacture of wicker cages with artificial birds illuminated by tiny battery-operated bulbs. Consumer interest was not great, however, and the Sadacca family accumulated a stockpile of unused material.

Fifteen-year-old Albert, who had only recently arrived from Madrid, read a newspaper story about a fire caused by a flaming Christmas tree. Prowling among the gadgets bought but not used by his relatives in their illuminated-bird business, the boy rigged up a string of little lights. They glowed so convincingly and so securely that older members of the family solemnly voted to abandon their former activity and go into the business of making and selling Christmas tree lights.

Albert V. Sadacca didn't achieve fame as a result of his invention; his name appears in few reference books. But Noma-World Wide Inc., the firm launched by a boy's fertile mind, now sells lights in a dozen countries and has an annual gross business of more than $10,000,000.

ZIPPER

Whitcomb L. Judson found the job of lacing and unlacing the high-top shoes worn in the 1890's a tedious job. Whether he had arthritis, simply didn't like the task, or was the recipient of a sudden, unsought inspiration is unknown. At any rate, he developed a "clasp locker or unlocker for shoes" that brought him a patent on August 29, 1893.

An acquaintance of Judson, Lewis Walker, was already so famous for his go-getting promotion of ideas that he was called by the honorary title of Colonel by most who knew him. In spite of the fact that his friend's clasp locker was complicated and clumsy, Colonel Walker saw great possibilities in a device that offered hope of liberation not only from shoestrings, but also from buttons, hooks and eyes, and other common fastening devices. Under the leadership of Walker the innovation brought about by Judson reached the market in 1896 as the Universal Fastener. It didn't create much enthusiasm.

A modified fastener that Judson called C-Curity, which sold for thirty-five cents and was anything but secure, began to appear in skirt plackets and trouser flies by 1910.

Westinghouse engineer Gideon Sundback gave up his old job in order to work for the Automatic Hook and Eye Company, where he devoted several years to improvement of Judson's final model. Sundback's Hookless No. 1 was a failure; his Hookless No. 2 brought a profit as a result of a military order. In 1923 a B. F. Goodrich Company executive, testing a Hookless No. 2, spontaneously dubbed it the zipper. Registered as a trade name, but now part of the general vocabulary, the term zipper has become attached to various slide fasteners.

Symbolic Characters

EMMY

In the early years of commercial television few performers devoted their full time to the medium. The growth of television was so rapid, however, that in surprisingly short order it was challenging the movie industry for the time and dollars of consumers.

Members of the Academy of Television Arts and Sciences decided that it would be appropriate to make some annual awards for outstanding performances and productions, so a female statuette was designed and named *Immy* after the technical term then in vogue, *image orthicon tube.*

"Image orthicon tube" was too big a mouthful for the general public. When it dropped from use, *Immy* no longer had meaning. So the name of the statuette was changed to Emmy about the time it became as highly prized as the Oscar of the film world.

SMOKEY THE BEAR

Men fighting a 1950 forest fire found a grizzly cub who had been separated from his mother. They rescued him and, unlike most grizzlies, he thrived in captivity. Association with the fire caused him to be named Smokey.

Eventually, Smokey was taken to the National Zoo in Washington. He became a favorite with visitors, and his picture often appeared in conservation magazines.

Officials of the U.S. Forest Service decided to make him the key character in a fire-prevention campaign. Congress became interested, and made it illegal to give his name to any other animal. So many drawings and sketches appeared that Smokey became synonymous with the campaign to prevent forest fires.

The life-span of the American black bear is about twenty-five to thirty years. Fearful that a national symbol would die unless Smokey fathered cubs, the Cooperative Forest Fire Prevention Committee in 1962 selected a mate for him. No cubs came along, however, so when Smokey was twenty the decision was reached to give him and his mate, Goldie, a little one to adopt. Regional wildlife groups were asked to submit candidates, preferably young male cubs "with fire experience." Inevitably the lucky cub selected was also dubbed "Smokey."

DEMOCRATIC DONKEY

In the tumultuous years after the Civil War, many persons in high office were subjected to stinging ridicule. Copperheads, or northern sympathizers with the southern cause, were particularly venomous in their attacks on Edwin M. Stanton.

Striking back at foes of Lincoln's Secretary of War, cartoonist Thomas Nast prepared a sketch that he entitled: "A Live Jackass Kicking a Dead Lion."

The dead lion was, of course, Stanton. Nast depicted a donkey in the act of giving the carcass a vigorous kick, with the U.S. eagle watching from a perch on a rock and with the U.S. Capitol in the background.

Immediately seized upon by opponents of Copperheads in particular and Democrats in general, the vivid symbol was an instant success. First used to convey ridicule, the donkey became a permanent fixture in American political life, not as a result of its choice by Democrats, but as an effect of its use by their opponents.

OSCAR

Beginning in the mid-1920's, individual members of California's growing motion picture colony proposed giving awards

75

for top performers and productions. Eventually the Academy of Motion Picture Arts and Sciences took the decisive step.

Actors, directors, and films released between August 1, 1927 and July 31, 1928 would be given "memorable awards."

It wasn't until May 16, 1929, that ceremonies were held and award winners were announced. Janet Gaynor was a recipient, along with Emil Jannings, who defeated Charlie Chaplin in competition for "best actor."

Each award winner received a handsome gold statuette. Unquestionably male, the figure resembled no one in particular. But it would add drama, promoters of the awards agreed, to give the little man a name. No one knows who suggested that he be called "Oscar."

The name stuck, however, and as prestige of the award mounted with the growth of the cinema industry, the winning of an Oscar became the supreme achievement in the careers of outstanding performers, directors, photographers, and writers.

AMERICAN EAGLE

Since the eagle is often regarded as the king of birds, it has been used as a symbol of royalty for many centuries. Babylonian and Persian as well as Roman rulers made use of it. So did soldiers of the Roman Republic; beginning in 87 B.C., a silver eagle with a thunderbolt in its claws was placed on the military standards borne at the head of the legions.

Casting about for a suitable national emblem, America's

founding fathers—most of them anyway—turned to the bald eagle that is native to this continent. On June 20, 1782 this bird was placed on the seal of the United States.

A few noted persons, including Benjamin Franklin, objected to the symbolic use of the eagle because of its links with ancient imperialism. Eighteen months after official action was taken, the Sage of Philadelphia was still grumbling.

In a famous letter to his daughter Sarah, written on January 26, 1784, Franklin said: "I wish the Bald Eagle had not been chosen as the Representative of our Country; he is a Bird of bad moral Character; like those among Men who live by Sharping and Robbing, he is generally poor, and often very lousy. The Turkey is a much more respectable Bird and withal a true original Native of America."

UNCLE SAM

Samuel Wilson served as the all-important inspector of provisions for U.S. troops in the War of 1812. At his Troy, New York, headquarters he was affectionately known as "Uncle Sam."

Since Uncle Sam and his subordinates branded "U.S." on all items that passed inspection, the coincidence of initials was too much to resist. At first on a local basis and then nationally, the name came to symbolize the Federal Government.

Forty years after Wilson had gained a kind of immortality through his nickname, U.S. and British shipowners became engaged in a fierce struggle. On this side of the Atlantic, federal officials stayed out of the matter. But in Britain high-ranking officers of the empire tried to intervene.

Cartoonist Frank Henry Temple Bellew drew a sketch to illustrate what he felt to be the issues and the antagonists. He showed John Bull actively at work assisting the Cunard Company, while Uncle Sam watched without going to the aid of a U.S. shipowner.

Bellew's cartoon had little impact on the shipping struggle; but the Uncle Sam whom he depicted in it was the prototype

77

of all cartoon figures symbolizing the national government of this country.

SUPERMAN

F. W. Nietzsche, gloomy German poet-philosopher whose ideas influenced both the German Empire and the Third Reich, believed men can perfect themselves by forcible self-assertion. In keeping with this idea, he devoted a great deal of time to books about *Übermensch*—the "overman" or "superman."

Jerry Siegel and Joe Shuster, teen-age hopefuls living in Cleveland, had never heard of Nietzsche or his doctrines. At eighteen they began trying to market a comic strip centering on an invincible hero, whom they called Superman.

Most publishers took one look and rejected the idea. It took five years for the author and illustrator to find a buyer. In 1938 Harry Donefeld was looking for an "action hero"—a cheap one. He bought sixty-four pages of Superman material at $10 a page—which included ownership of the coined name.

Superman made his first appearance in the obscure little *Action Comics* in the spring of 1938. An instant hit, he became a valuable literary property. The hero who fought evil dressed in tights and a cape came to personify all fictional characters who are simultaneously human and more-than-human.

78

REPUBLICAN ELEPHANT

Four years after the Democratic donkey was born, Thomas Nast drew for *Harper's Weekly* a cartoon depicting inner chaos in the Republican Party. Published on November 7, 1874, it borrowed from the style of ancient fables and informed the public that "An Ass, having put on the Lion's skin, roamed about the Forest, and amused himself by frightening all the foolish Animals he met with in his wanderings."

The ass was, of course, the Democratic Party to most who saw the cartoon. This despite the fact that in it the animal was labelled "N. Y. Herald."

Numerous timid animals were depicted as running from the ass in a lion's skin, while a berserk elephant labelled "Republican vote" was tossing platform planks in every direction.

Republican divisiveness centered largely about the possibility that U. S. Grant would seek a third term. Though Nast was rebuking the party rather than complimenting it, his elephant made such an impact that it became the permanent symbol of the Republican Party.

STORK

Ancient Roman myths say that on one occasion many gods and goddesses were permitted to choose birds and animals to be associated with them. According to the venerable legend the goddess of love, Venus, chose the stork.

Especially in northwestern Europe the stork is a useful scavenger. A migrant, the big bird flies long distances twice each year. Suddenly appearing "out of nowhere" as nesting time approaches, it is regarded with superstitious awe. So it is natural that the storks' building their nest upon one's house should be considered a sign of good luck.

In Germany, Holland, Norway, Denmark, and other countries the bird that brings good luck and shows up annually in time to prepare a place for little ones soon to be hatched was almost inevitably linked with the mystery of birth.

When children asked where babies come from, they were

79

told: "The stork brings them." Credibility was enhanced by the fact that many of the birds seemed big enough to transport human infants.

Strongly established in northwestern Europe over a period of centuries, the symbol has spread around the world. In many regions where white storks are never seen, these birds still continue to be regarded as "bringers of babies."

THREE WISE MONKEYS

Terse sayings such as those found in the biblical book of Proverbs are common to many religions. At least as early as the eighth century, many Buddhists were familiar with the injunction: "See no evil, hear no evil, speak no evil."

Somewhere in China, artisans decided to translate that commandment into symbolic form. Because monkeys were common as well as agile, these animals were selected to convey the message without words.

Three monkeys perched close together were laboriously fashioned by hand. One animal held his paws over his eyes; the second covered his ears; the third held both paws, crossed, upon his mouth.

From China the carvings were introduced into Japan. There Westerners found them when the Land of the Rising Sun established contact with European nations. An instant hit with persons who knew nothing of Buddhist teachings but appreciated the message of the carved monkeys, they have since spread throughout the world.

SACRED COW

Gautama, the Buddha, abhorred the shedding of blood. One of the cardinal principles he impressed upon his followers exhorted: "Do not slaughter animals; let them go free!" As a result of this principle, all good Buddhists are vegetarians.

Most animals used as food by Western man are relatively scarce in the Orient. But in some regions, notably India, cattle thrive. They roam about the countryside and the streets of cities at will. They consume enormous amounts of food badly needed for India's underfed population. They contribute to filth and the spread of disease. Still, a faithful Buddhist would be aghast at the idea of killing a cow.

Westerners who visit India and become acquainted with this aspect of Indian life return home practically foaming at the mouth. Even today, agricultural experts insist that the "sacred cow" is a major obstacle to India's program of self-improvement.

Frequent discussion about the animal that is venerated in such fashion that it is a burden to the people of India led to adoption of the sacred cow as a symbol for a person, idea, or institution treated as immune from reasonable criticism.

JOHN DOE

Under English common law, matters involving the leasing of land often became extremely involved. Frequently the courts were faced with a dilemma. In certain kinds of ejectment the leaseholder was treated as the plaintiff, but the action might be instituted by the landlord. On great estates the names of refractory tenants weren't always known.

No papers could be drawn up, however, without stipulating the names of the parties involved. As a legal fiction, to get around difficulties involving cases in which one or more names weren't known to the court, someone coined the name John Doe. It served so well as a symbol for an unknown plaintiff that Richard Roe was adopted as a substitute for the name of a defendant not known to the court.

These sham names, British attorneys explain, were used for generations in order to "save certain niceties of the law."

In the process of appearing on many a writ, both Richard Roe and John Doe were permanently imprinted upon English speech. Partly because he was named more often, partly because his name appeared first if several were listed, John Doe became the more famous of the two nonexistent men.

81

Until rulings by the U.S. Supreme Court outlawed many police practices it was common for officers hunting a man of unknown identity to secure a "John Doe writ" that enabled them to arrest any suspect they might discover.

JOLLY ST. NICK

Santa Claus (a variation of St. Nicholas) is not a modern creation. At various times and in limited regions he has been linked with Christmas for many centuries.

Until 1823, however, he did not take on the traits we link with Jolly St. Nick. Before that time he was often portrayed as lean and lank, and stories about him suggested that he was a bit grumpy.

This image changed with publication of a single poem. Clement Clarke Moore wrote "A Visit from St. Nicholas" in December, 1822, for the amusement of a sick child. When it was published the next year as " 'Twas the Night Before Christmas," he didn't permit his name to be attached to it.

More than any other Christmas poem produced in the English-speaking world, it caught the imagination of the general public. Because Moore portrayed the Spirit of Christmas as a jolly little man who shook like a bowl full of jelly when he laughed from his perch on a sled pulled by reindeer, Santa Claus ceased to be regarded as glum and came to symbolize the spontaneous gaiety that marks Christmas at its best.

JOHN BULL

Scottish writer-physician John Arbuthnot took great interest in political affairs. To him the greatest villain in the British Empire was the Duke of Marlborough.

Arbuthnot attacked the powerful English leader in a satire that he called *The History of John Bull*. For his title he probably borrowed from the colloquial speech of his native country where every Englishman was about as welcome as a snorting bull.

Publication of the pamphlet had no significant impact upon the influence of Arbuthnot's target. But throughout the English-speaking world it was reprinted and quoted with glee. As a result, John Bull became the humorous personification of the British people.

Cartoonists still depict him essentially as described by the Scottish physician. John Bull is stout, red-faced, bluff, and short-tempered. Decidedly rustic in appearance, he wears leather breeches and top boots. A bulldog stands at his heels, and he carries a stout oak cudgel—ready to whack any nation (such as wee Scotland) that dares to get in his way.

WHITE ELEPHANT

Long ago in both Burma and Siam the rare white elephant was regarded as a sacred animal. Rulers of both lands considered their grandest title to be "King of the White Elephant."

It was a capital offense to injure one of these sacred animals. Kings spared no expense in caring for their small herds.

An ancient story, transmitted orally for centuries, tells of a king of Siam who devised a ruse to ruin powerful foes without overt attack. He simply gave a white elephant to any man whose power he wished to break. The cost of maintaining the animal was enough to break even a wealthy lord—but he could neither refuse the royal gift nor dispose of the white elephant after he got it.

If the story is based on historical incidents, scholars have been unable to identify the ruler or rulers who launched the practice of giving white elephants. Historical or not, the tale captured the imagination of Westerners and even in the electronic age "white elephant" symbolizes a possession a person can't easily dispose of but really doesn't want.

PHOENIX

Druggists with a sense of history still display an emblem that portrays a bird no one ever saw—the phoenix. The bird's association with prescription shops grew out of the fact that the phoenix was used as a symbol by many medieval alchemists.

Arabian mythology described numerous rare and unusual creatures, but none was more exotic than the phoenix. Just one bird lived at any given time. When the phoenix felt death approaching, it flew to an inaccessible mountaintop and built itself a nest of spices. After singing a mournful song, the bird flapped its wings so forcefully that its nest caught fire. Burned to ashes, the fabulous phoenix was reborn from its funeral pyre and began another cycle of existence.

Shakespeare and many other notable writers were intrigued with the story of the bird that symbolized "something out of nothing." Neither they nor others had any idea, however, that the creature from mythology would give its name to the largest city of Arizona.

Games

DECK OF FIFTY-TWO CARDS

Early Chinese packs of cards consisted of thirty cards divided into three suits of nine each, plus three single cards of special power. Predominance of the number three in this pattern suggests that belief in its occult power was a factor in the development of such a deck.

Playing cards probably didn't reach Europe before the thirteenth century; a famous dialogue on games by Petrarch (1278) makes no mention of them. By the late fourteenth century they were known in France, Italy, and England.

Early decks probably consisted simply of a set of already familiar *tarrochi*, or tarot cards. Used in fortune-telling and in divination, the standard set consisted of seventy-eight cards divided into four suits. Contemporary interest in the borderline occult has led to revival of divination by means of tarot cards.

Reduction of the deck to a standard fifty-two cards was almost certainly a concession to the fact that there are just fifty-two weeks in a year. No one knows when or where this innovation was tried. Players quickly discovered, however, that the "simplified pack" made for faster and better games; all efforts to add to or substract from the deck that made players think of the weeks comprising a year have failed.

KINGS, QUEENS, AND JACKS

Simultaneously with the reduction in the size of packs of cards from seventy-eight to fifty-two little pasteboards, there were a number of experiments aimed at improving the game by introducing new values for some cards. Kings, queens, and knaves (symbolic of servants) appeared on French playing cards that were used about 1450.

Since then, there have been many attempts to make cards "more democratic" or better suited to circumstances of the moment. During the French Revolution, men like Voltaire, Rousseau, and La Fontaine replaced the kings while great figures from mythology and history replaced queens and knaves.

Some countries were adamant in their refusal to honor ladies by placing queens on cards. Even today, most packs bought in Spain and in Latin America are all male.

English and American manufacturers have experimented with a great variety of designs. These range from commemorative packs celebrating the downfall of the Spanish Armada to historical ones that honor U.S. presidents and national heroes.

In spite of all but universal repudiation of government by monarchy, all attempts to rid cards of symbols that point to royalty have failed. With the medieval knave altered to modern jack, practically all cards used in the English-speaking world perpetuate French symbols of respect for rulers and their ladies.

FOUR SUITS

Chinese cards of the earliest sort were divided into only three varieties, called "suits" by modern players. Veneration for the mystical number three was overshadowed by the fact that the year has four seasons. It isn't certain whether the use of four suits became general before or after the size of a pack was standardized so that cards symbolized weeks of the year.

All early cards were hand-painted, and the symbols used on them varied widely. Italians preferred cups, swords, money, and batons; French favored hearts, diamonds, spades, and clubs; north Europeans frequently used hearts, bells, leaves (or "greens"), and acorns.

The materials used varied as widely as the symbols. Many cards were bits of hand-rubbed leather that bore elaborate designs. Some were engraved by hand on silver or even on mother-of-pearl. A handmade five of diamonds once sold for about $15,000—because Holbein had decorated it with a portrait of the Duchess of Norfolk.

Even after printing came into vogue, costly sets were produced. One of them gave a pictorial history of England from the time of Queen Anne to 1706 and used portraits of leading political figures for the knaves.

General (though not universal) adoption of four suits made up of hearts, diamonds, spades, and clubs is a tribute to the fervor with which French devotees played and the zeal with which they urged the adoption of symbols first widely used in their land.

CHESS

The beginnings of chess are lost in antiquity. Development of the game has been credited to the Chinese as well as to the Hindus of India. Less plausible traditions assert that it was invented by the Egyptians, the Jews, the Greeks, and the Romans.

One thing is certain: chess was played by Persian noblemen at least as early as the middle of the sixth century. Three independent sources (Persian, Arabic, and Sanskrit documents) corroborate this fact. According to all three, the game was introduced into Persia from India—where it may have been in vogue much earlier.

Chaturanga, or "a complete army," was the native Indian name for the collection of chessmen, or tokens. Chess is clearly a military game in origin. The traditional Indian use of four kinds of troops (infantry, cavalry, charioteers, and warriors on elephant back) is reflected in the four kinds of chessmen who still struggle with one another under the command of a king and queen (originally a king and his viceroy).

There is no reliable evidence that chess was played in ancient China, though sporadic encounters between Hindus and Chinese may have led the latter to develop playing cards as a substitute for chess.

87

Originating in India and spreading westward into Persia, the game reached Europe by way of Arabia.

PAWN

Armies fielded by ancient Hindu kings included a great many more infantrymen than mounted warriors. Men on foot were not only more numerous than those who rode into battle; they were considered the least powerful and therefore the most expendable.

Reflection of this military philosophy is clearly preserved in modern chess, where pawns outnumber all other subordinate pieces combined.

Pawn, today's title for the least-powerful chesspiece is derived from a medieval French term for foot soldier; this in turn represents a garbled form of a much earlier Hindu title for "attendant," or infantryman, whose principal duty was to guard a man of superior rank mounted on a war animal or riding in a chariot.

The significance of the pawn—a piece any player will gladly sacrifice in order to capture a more powerful member of his opponent's force—supports the view that chess was developed in order to give instruction in the theory of war.

QUEEN, BISHOP, ROOK

The role and importance of pawns, or infantrymen, has changed little through centuries of chess-playing. Today's knight points quite clearly to the ancient Hindu cavalryman.

The rook (or castle) used in European sets gives no hint that it has taken the place of the elephant used by oriental players.

Substitution of a powerful bishop for the chariot that was used in earlier sets reflects the power politics of medieval Italy, where prestige of churchmen was second only to that of the king.

Italy is also credited with having transformed the Hindu

viceroy, second in command to the king, into the queen, most powerful of all aggressive figures on the chessboard. While preserving its essential character as a war game, modern chess (largely shaped by Italian influence) attempts to depict a kingdom and its classes of citizens rather than an oriental army.

WHIST

Still enjoying moderate popularity in England, whist was once *the* card game. Its original name, whisk, may have stemmed from the fact that it was customary to pull out or whisk away all the deuces before the cards were shuffled.

Tradition asserts that whist was invented in order to help members of parliament relax after they had spent the day with affairs of state. Whether that is the case or not, it did originate somewhere in Britain and rose to national popularity during the eighteenth century. It is one of the few card games borrowed by the French from the English.

Horace Walpole, whose literary reputation is based largely on some 2,700 letters that he wrote during a period of sixty years, devoted one of the letters to whist—which he branded as "one of England's dullest possessions."

Contemporary connoisseurs of card games are inclined to agree with Walpole. Still, it was whist which spurred the first edition of one of the most famous of modern manuals. Edmund Hoyle was dismayed at the fact whist was played in a variety of ways, so he drew up and printed a *Short Treatise* expounding what he considered to be the proper rules of the game. First issued in 1742, Hoyle's laws for whist continued to be regarded as authoritative until 1864. By then, "according to Hoyle" had come to be the equivalent of "correct." Present-day manuals of play, which still have Hoyle's name attached to them, devote less than 1 percent of their pages to whist.

RUSSIAN ROULETTE

The most deadly of all games didn't originate in Russia and, unlike roulette, offers no payoff.

It got its start in 1808. That year, an impetuous student at Cambridge University picked up a pistol, held it to his head, and pulled the trigger. He had no idea whether or not it was loaded, but since it was a single-shot weapon he was making a fifty-fifty bet that the pistol was empty. That bet proved to be wrong.

Matters would have stopped with a temporary and local flurry of talk about this rash act had it not been that the game's victim was a roommate of one George Gordon.

On the death of a great uncle, Gordon succeeded to a family title and became Lord Byron. Byron gave a full description of the college tragedy in his famous memoirs. A copy of Byron's book fell into the hands of a Russian novelist who in 1839 wrote a noted short story, *The Fatalist*, in which the action turned on a repetition of the fatal performance given by Byron's college friend.

Western readers who first heard of the "game" from Lermontov's story naturally dubbed this life-or-death gamble as "Russian." Annually, two or three Americans die as a result of playing it despite the fact that the odds are now much better than those of the English college youth who took a 50/50 chance. A revolver with five empty chambers and one that contains a live bullet offers to the player an eighty-four to sixteen chance of walking away alive.

BRIDGE

Whist players who became bored with the game made many attempts to improve it. One such variant, played by British diplomats and army officers in Constantinople, was based upon a Near-Eastern game that had been played for decades without attracting more than regional interest.

As modified by the British this form of whist employed a vocal formula. The one declaring could say "biritch" in lieu of declaring trumps. This meant that the hands should be played without trumps. An additional complicating factor was introduced with the agreement that the signal should also mean that each odd trick would count ten points.

Brought back to London as biritch or Russian whist, this derivative of the older game soon gained so many followers that conventional whist was overshadowed.

Though there are written references to biritch that appeared as early as 1886, no scholar knows precisely what the word meant in its original context. An 1894 volume that offered a *Pocket Guide to Bridge* dealt with "Russian whist." This form of the game was superseded by "auction bridge," considered more lively than "dummy bridge," and widely popular before 1910.

There have been some relatively minor changes in rules for play since 1910, but bridge itself remains unchallenged as the dominant card game of the Western world.

BACKGAMMON

At least as early as the tenth century Arabs took great interest in the game of nard, played with draughtsmen on a special board and ruled by fate (in the form of the throwing of dice).

Arabs probably developed their game from "the twelve-line game" of Romans. Plato's *Republic* preserves one of the few written references to this ancient diversion.

Christians who set out to recapture the Holy Land from the infidels in the time of the Crusades learned nard from their foes. Returning home, they modified the game a bit and it became modern backgammon. Current popularity of backgammon dates from the early seventeenth century.

CHECKERS

Games that employed the basic principles of checkers (called draughts in Britain) have been played for about four thousand years. Archaeological evidence includes an Egyptian vase that depicts a lion and an antelope playing a form of checkers, plus part of the actual checkerboard used by Queen Hatshepsut about 1600 B.C.

In the *Odyssey* Homer describes one of the most famous of all checker games. Penelope's suitors played it while trying to persuade the beautiful woman that Ulysses was dead and that she'd better choose one of them as her husband.

Literary evidence indicates that this very early Greek form of the game employed a board with twenty-five squares; each player had five men. Numerous other variants appeared in Italy, Spain, Turkey, Russia, and India. Boards with sixty-four squares appeared during the seventeenth century and soon nosed out all competitors.

Widespread traditions to the effect that checkers evolved as a simplified form of chess for use by persons lacking the skill and patience to play the more complicated game are without foundation.

POKER

Many experts think the old French game of Gilet (itself borrowed from Italy) is the seedbed from which the many varieties of modern poker sprang. This much is certain: it was first played in French territory in the New World. Whether it developed in and around New Orleans or was brought there by soldiers of fortune, no one knows.

There is no written reference to poker prior to an 1834 description of a game played on a river steamer. Published under the title *Exposure of the Arts and Miseries of Gambling,* the account had absolutely no effect upon the triumphant sweep of the game throughout the frontier territory in the United States.

More than any other game, ancient or modern, poker has enriched everyday speech. A full list of its contributions would become tiresome; some of them are: poker face, ante up, pass the buck, ace in the hole, stand pat, chip in, and four-flusher. Contemporary editions of *Hoyle* describe special kinds of poker that range from "stud" to "peek," from "spit in the ocean" to "wild widow."

Though there were already plenty of pastimes designed to help redistribute wealth when French-American adventurers concocted the new game, none of them had the precise flair that makes poker unique. Compounded from approximately equal portions of luck, skill with cards, and proficiency in psychology, poker when played without a joker has 2,598,960 potential hands.

MONOPOLY

Though outdistanced on the long haul by chess and several card games, for a period of nearly twenty years the contest merchandised under the registered trade name of Monopoly was the most popular of all parlor games.

Significantly, Monopoly emerged in the United States during the depression. It was the brainchild of an unemployed plumber who, like Walter Mitty, found it hard to distinguish between reality and his fantasies. Juggling homemade props on a kitchen table, the plumber dreamed of gaining one monopoly after another until he was the head of a financial empire.

Parker Brothers bought the game from its inventor, offered it to a public desperately concerned with finances, and, in the first generation it was on the market, sold an estimated thirty million sets.

MINIATURE GOLF

Golf's enormous land requirements brought frustration to many early U.S. enthusiasts. Some of them went so far as to develop courses with fewer than nine holes and with distance from tee-off to hole greatly reduced. Such courses didn't satisfy real golfers, but were too difficult for rank amateurs.

Promoter John G. Carter of Chattanooga, Tennessee, had an inspiration late in the 1920's. Legend says his idea was born as a result of attending a Tom Thumb wedding staged in connection with a local civic celebration.

Carter deliberately scrapped all attempts to offer conventional golf on a small scale. He built a "Tom Thumb" course and registered the trade name, stipulated that players could use only putters, but devised a system of obstacles and hazards.

Anticipating the trend toward synthetic materials, Carter fashioned his greens with a compound of cottonseed hulls dyed green. His "Tom Thumb" franchise prospered briefly but was soon overwhelmed by competitors who offered sweethearts, families with small children, and persons bored with other forms of recreation an opportunity to play "miniature golf."

DICE

Though now associated with activities that range from family parlor games to bigtime gambling, dice originated as a response to man's universal desire to probe into the future. Many forms of divination have been practiced in practically all cultures; of these, various ways of "casting lots" in order to learn the degrees of fate rank close to the top in usage and in importance.

Some archaeologists think that the first dice were knuckle-bones from the hind legs of sheep and other domestic animals. These were oblong, rather than square.

The Greek writer Sophocles claims that Palamedes invented dice to divert the fighting men who had much idle time on their hands during the siege of Troy. This couldn't possibly have been the case; the siege took place sometime just before or after 1500 B.C. and archaeologists have found dice in sites nearly two thousands years older.

Hebrews used a sacred cube (of which no example has ever been found, and about whose inscriptions or symbols nothing is known) to ask questions of Jehovah. A pair of these cubes, called *Urim and Thummim* and used only by chief priests, could be relied upon to give yes or no answers to questions.

So linked with divine forces and with fate, cubes with sets of dots on their faces became the most widely used of all devices considered spokesmen from whose verdict there is no appeal. Whether the issue is the movement of a playing piece in a children's game or ownership of a horde of chips on a gambling table, the dice will decide.

CROQUET

At least as early as the thirteenth century, idlers in the south of France became enamored of a game that involved knocking balls about on a stretch of level turf. Known as *paille maille*, it was later adopted by the English as *pall-mall*. Island enthusiasts devoted so much time and attention to the game that its name was attached to the famous Pall Mall Street in London.

Many an American shopping center with a spacious mall owes a linguistic debt to the game favored by courtiers and gentlewomen of Britain.

About 1850 a group of French devotees who spent a period in Ireland taught the game to their hosts. Tradition says that within two years the Irish had added more balls and hoops and had designed a mallet with a slightly curved head. Too proud to use a French name for their game, the Irish entitled it "crokis."

First played on the lawn of Lord Lonsdale's mansion in 1852, the game quickly reached England and won a following among players of the less intricate pall-mall. Public demand induced a toymaker to convert his shop to the manufacture of the gear needed to play the "Irish" game. With its name modified enough to give it a bit of a Continental flair, croquet was standardized during the 1860's and from its base in Britain has spread around the world.

BILLIARDS

French sportsmen passionately fond of bowling were deprived of this recreation on many cold, wet days. Some of them conceived the idea of bringing their game indoors and playing it on an artificial green. The *bille*, or curved cue, with which early players struck balls probably gave billiards its name.

Long limited to persons of wealth with time on their hands, the game was played at least as early as 1450. It crossed the channel and won many devotees in Britain. Her prowess with the cue made Mary, Queen of Scots, the talk of sportsmen throughout the island kingdom.

Shakespeare erroneously described Cleopatra, bored by the absence of Antony, as proposing a game of billiards to while away the time. While that reference is anachronistic, many of England's greatest writers have penned lines in praise of the game.

Various shades of green felt were used upon early tables, and some of them were covered with blue. Prince Leopold of Hohenzollern (1835-1905) is credited with having introduced the pure olive green that quickly became standard.

Until comparatively recently, billiard balls were made of ivory. Since they weren't uniform while "green," ivory balls were stored in incubators before being placed on the market. The shortage of this essential material for one of the world's most fascinating games spurred development of the first man-made plastic (see "Celluloid").

LONDON BRIDGE

Children of many nations play games that involve falling bridges. The English version that emphasizes the awe in which the original London Bridge was held varies from games of other cultures only in superficial details.

At least one anthropologist and historian, Henry Bett, has ventured to explain the origin of these games on the basis of the fact that sacrificial victims were frequently buried alive in the foundations of bridges in order to appease evil spirits.

This conjecture, which is beyond verification, overlooks a far simpler explanation. Even the best of modern bridges are not absolutely safe; early ones built of wood plus stone and iron were notoriously dangerous. Anytime a bridge collapsed with persons on it, lives were sure to be endangered if not lost.

That being the case, the children's game may represent a reenactment of tragedy—with consequences of structural failure reduced to momentary capture.

PACHISI

Weavers of ancient India, who were forever experimenting with new patterns, developed a particularly unusual one fashioned after designs drawn on the ground with a stick. Three rows of eight squares were placed around a center square. Using this pattern, the ancient game of *pachisi* was played on both impromptu outdoor courts and miniature ones made for indoor use.

Probably named for a term meaning "twenty-five" since the highest possible throw in the game is twenty-five, pachisi was first played with cowrie shells (now replaced by dice).

For centuries pachisi was *the* game of India.

Akbar the Great, sixteenth-century emperor of Hindustan, was an ardent player. He was so ardent, in fact, that when the sumptuous palace at his new capital of Fatehpur Sikri was built the ruler demanded that the architects provide him with the world's finest place to play pachisi. They complied by using red and white squares for the court of the zenana, making it possible for Akbar to play pachisi using sixteen young slaves from his harem as playing pieces.

The emperors of Delhi imitated this magnificent style in their palace at Agra. Present-day Americans, many of whom still play the game virtually as it was played a thousand years ago, usually employ machine-made boards and playing pieces. *Parcheesi* is a registered trademark for a game that has been modified slightly from the one Akbar the Great played when he wished to divert his mind from affairs of state.

BINGO

According to verbal traditions transmitted in Italy for centuries, bingo was invented before 1520 by a nobleman of that country. Benedetto Gentile, credited with having developed the game, taught it to high-ranking officers in the armies of King Francis I. These men, in turn, took the diversion with them when they returned to France.

As a rule, any story crediting one person with development of a complex game is suspect—though Monopoly is an exception. Genoese nobleman Gentile probably borrowed from far older sources and made adaptations that caused his game to surge into international popularity.

Early French players gave specific and sometimes picturesque names to many numbers used in bingo. When the game invaded Britain, this practice continued and resulted in such labels as "Kelly's eye" for zero and "clicketty click" for sixty-six.

Members of the international set who spent much of their time on cruise steamers took to the game like ducks to water. For a period, however, they called it housey-housey or tombola (a variant of a popular Italian name). Bingo, long used as a slang term for brandy, didn't come into use as the name of the game until nineteenth-century players found that a sudden win is as exhilarating as a glass of soda water with a dash of liquid bingo.

Sports

HOCKEY

For several centuries English sportsmen have played hockey on hard turf during cold weather. Scots use the same playing surface for their game of shinty. But hurley, the Irish equivalent of the ball-and-stick contest, is played on the hard, sandy seashore.

Just when and where players first took to the ice, no one knows. Some sixteenth- and seventeenth-century paintings from the Low Countries show contestants gliding about on frozen ponds and lakes. From the same root that gave us "to bandy about" as a label for discussing a subject from all sides, the helter-skelter game on ice was long called *bandy.*

It didn't become hockey until relatively recent times. Many clues point to a link with an Old French term for a shepherd's staff. Whether that was the source or not, it's fairly certain that the game is named for the crooked stick used in playing it. An account of 1527 refers to "hockie stickes or staves"—at that time still used chiefly on land.

Abundant water and long, hard winters in Canada and the northern United States brought ice hockey into its own. A good hawky, or playing stick, was prized as early as the 1830's. But no recognized code of rules governing the sport was drawn up until 1881.

That code was the work of Canadian enthusiasts who supported the Victoria Hockey Club, acting in cooperation with Montreal's McGill University. Since its birth, in 1881, as an organized sport, ice hockey has practically made field hockey obsolete.

RINK

Renc, an Old French term for "row," was long used to designate the ground space on which a row of persons competed by riding, racing, or jumping. From this usage it was a natural transition to apply the label to a stretch of ice marked off for curling.

Robert Burns, Scotland's national poet, was familiar with such a surface. In his "Tam Samson's Elegy" Burns described a skater who roared up the rink like Jehu, a famous Old Testament chariot driver.

Burns was describing a grim contestant, not a pleasure skater. The transfer of "rink" to any stretch of ice for skating and then to a wood or asphalt floor for roller skating is a recent development due to the impact of hockey.

With the rise of professional hockey the rink has become all-important. Size and lighting are obvious variables; some veteran players insist that their game is affected by the temperature of the ice. Still gaining in popularity as a spectator sport, pro hockey now has so many followers that few major cities are without at least one rink.

PUCK

Puck, a long lost north European term for "to hit or strike" gave its name to anything that was habitually struck.

In early versions of hockey, the puck (constantly assailed by blows from every direction) was usually a wooden cricket ball.

Introduction of India-rubber into the Western world made it possible to produce a rolling piece with considerable bounce. Such a puck added immensely to the speed of hockey. In 1894 a writer for *Outing* magazine became ecstatic after seeing the action on the ice. "These men," he wrote, "handle the little innocent rubber puck as Paderewski handles the black keys of a piano!"

Tradition credits the invention of the modern puck to players at McGill University. Sometime prior to 1879 hockey players there are said to have substituted a rubber ball for the traditional wooden one. It added plenty of bounce—too much, in fact. Ingenious players therefore sliced off the top and bottom of the ball in order to form a flat rubber disk—the ancestor of the modern machine-made puck.

"TELEGRAPHING"

Professional hockey is indebted for one of its commonly used terms—somewhat indirectly, mind you—to a now-forgotten French military engineer. Wrestling with the problem of communicating at a distance, he rigged up a set of posts with movable arms. From the Greek word for "that which writes" this learned fellow called his semaphore signal "the telegraph."

Naturally the vivid name was attached to other communicating devices—including the scoreboard used in cricket. Samuel Morse borrowed it to name his magnetic signaling device nearly half a century after "telegraph" had entered the vocabulary of rough-and-tumble handlers of the puck.

Today a player given to transmitting telltale signals to his opponent, or telegraphing, may wind up on the bench; if he doesn't lick the habit he may not get his contract renewed.

GOLF

Sir W. G. Simpson, a noted authority on the history of sports, traces the beginning of golf to a sheep pasture in

Fifeshire, Scotland. In order to pass the time, Simpson theorizes, a shepherd knocked pebbles through the air with his crook. When one stone happened to fall into a rabbit hole, a friend challenged him to repeat the shot.

This tongue-in-cheek explanation delves into circumstances that possibly launched one of the world's most popular sports. Whatever may have been the exact pattern of events that shaped the game, golf was first played in Scotland and its organized rules were drawn up at the Royal and Ancient Golf Club of St. Andrews.

Scholars have had no end of trouble with the origin of the name of the game now played by millions. Popular accounts often skim over difficulties and trace it to the Dutch *kolf* (club).

There are obstacles in the way of this explanation. Golf was played centuries before any Dutch sport involved the use of a kolf. And there is no evidence that the Scots ever used an initial *c* or *k* in speaking of their national pastime.

Earliest players probably dipped into their store of unwritten slang to name the new sport. By the time English novelist Tobias Smollett visited Scotland in the 1760's the title had become standardized. Smollett was greatly interested in learning that "hard by, in the fields called the Links, the citizens of Edinburgh divert themselves at a game called Golf."

STANCE

Italian musicians of the Middle Ages modified a Latin term for "stopping place" and shaped *stanza* to indicate a segment of a composition that required a full stop. Passing through Old French and again being modified when adopted into sixteenth-century English, the musical term for a stopping place entered the speech of workmen as "stance."

To take one's place at a stance was equivalent to being at a standstill, so it was natural to use the much traveled word to name a platform on which a person stood. Stances were common fixtures on warships as well as in mines and factories.

No one knows precisely when the word passed from industry

into sport, but the transition was not made until late in the last century. Adopted as just the right label to fill a gap in the vocabulary of golf, it entered print in 1897. That year a writer for the British magazine *Outing* solemnly informed his readers that "the grip, the stance, the swing, together make up what they call a good style."

Most large public libraries include an entire shelf of volumes on golf; most of the books agree in stressing the importance of the stance—but vary widely in their prescriptions for a winning one.

LINKS

Possibly through the influence of Old English *hlinc* (to lean), "leaning" or sloping ground took that title before the tenth century.

The terrain of Scotland is such that one can go only a short distance along the seacoast before coming upon a gently leaning piece of ground covered with turf. No one knows whether or not golf was first played within sight of the ocean. But characteristics of shoreland were almost certainly utilized from the very beginning of the game. It was the hoary title for "sloping ground" that came to designate the playing area.

In golf, the term has rarely been used in the singular. This suggests but doesn't positively prove that the earliest games were played on a series of connecting links.

Development of a new course suitable for championship play now involves the outlay of hundreds of thousands of dollars. Part of the initial investment goes to make certain that areas of sloping ground are strategically located within the links.

TROPHY ROOM

When an ancient Greek military commander put an enemy to flight, he usually erected a victory memorial. From *trophe* (turning, defeating) a marker commemorating the turn of tide in a battle was called *tropaion*.

The Romans who conquered the Greeks continued both the

practice of erecting monuments and using a special name for them. Passing from Latin into English as a result of the work of fifteenth-century scholars who translated ancient military records, the symbol of victory became known as a "trophy." Anything regarded as a prize in war naturally bore that special title.

But Scotsmen and Englishmen took their sports almost as seriously as their battles, and the practice of awarding a trophy for victory in competition became common. Victors who competed in other sporting events were receiving trophies long before any were awarded to golfers. Nowhere, however, has the basic idea had greater impact than among devotees of the links. The world's first formal trophy room was established at the birthplace of modern golf, the Royal and Ancient Golf Club of St. Andrews, Scotland.

CADDY

Mary, Queen of Scots (1542-1567), is famous as the first woman known to have played golf. Since the queen was educated in France it was natural for her to use *cadet* (young fellow) to refer to the youth who carried her clubs. She gave the word its French pronunciation, but fellow golfers who borrowed it from Her Majesty quickly slurred it into a Scottish form, caddy.

The impact of golf talk was so great that in the vicinity of Edinburgh a male of any age who waited for chance employment as porter or messenger was given the title of the clubbearer. Golf bags came into general use late in the nineteenth century, but many caddies of that era retained the habit of carrying clubs under their arms.

It would be impossible to list all the great sportsmen who got their start by working as caddies. Gene Sarazen was caddy number 99 at Apawamis Golf Club in Harrison, New York. John B. Nelson, "the mechanical man" of the 1930's, earned seventy-five cents a round as a caddy at Glen Garden in Fort Worth. Ben Hogan worked for sixty-five cents a round—plus tips!

Advent of the motorized golf cart has put caddies out of business on most public courses. Even in the finest of private clubs the once essential "young fellow" who carried clubs is seldom seen except in cup competition.

SKIS

Pre-Germanic hunters in Scandinavia used long pieces of wood to glide over snow. Digging in a bog at Hoting, Sweden, workmen found such gear in a level believed to date from about 2500 B.C. At Rodoy, Norway, a rock carving from 2000 B.C. depicts an elk hunter whose feet are equipped with devices remarkably like those seen in space-age winter resorts.

Very early, Norwegians employed the word *ski* to name "a billet of cleft wood" used in moving over snow. Improvements in the sporting gear came slowly, and the Norwegian name didn't win ready acceptance among persons of English descent.

Showshoe Thomson, the famous U.S. mailman whose route lay in the High Sierras, was a native of Norway. But all his life he referred to his footgear as "the pads" or "snowshoes."

Improvements in woodworking that made it possible for amateurs to have snow gear that is pointed and curved at one end, with the edges rounded, coincided roughly with the adoption of the Norwegian label. Now machine made from materials not available to the workmen who produced early "gliding billets," modern skis are precision instruments that are often carefully adapted to the height and weight of the person who will use them to conquer the icy slopes.

COURT TENNIS

Two French monks with time on their hands began idly knocking a ball around a monastery courtyard with crude wooden paddles. That was about seven hundred years ago. From this diversion sprang one of the most complicated of all sports: court tennis. At least, that's the story the French give.

Regardless of whether or not original players were monks, the game did begin as a courtyard contest. Eventually it became the most popular sport in France. King Louis X played so hard that exertion in a match contributed to his death.

Limited chiefly to kings and courtiers, the game attracted such adherents as Henry VIII of England, Louis XIII of, France, and Philip IV of Spain. Both the Duke of Wellington and Napoleon played—but had they been matched against one another it would have been a dull contest; Wellington was far faster and more accurate.

By no means dead, court tennis is still played by a few thousand persons with plenty of time and money. A modern court is a highly stylized version of a medieval courtyard, and can't be built for less than $250,000. No wonder there are just twenty-seven places in the world where devotees of court tennis can display their skill: sixteen in Britain, seven in the United States, two in France, and two in Australia.

LAWN TENNIS

Court tennis had been played for several centuries before anyone thought of adapting the game so that it could be played out of doors at relatively low cost. Several adaptations of "the royal sport" appeared almost simultaneously in the nineteenth century.

One of the pioneers was a career man in the British Army, Walter C. Wingfield. Then a captain in an artillery company, Wingfield made no significant changes in ball, net, and bat (or racquet). But he had stunning ideas about the shape of "a proper court on which to divert one's self in the open air."

As designed by the Englishman, an outdoor tennis court was shaped somewhat like an hourglass. Obviously it wouldn't do to bestow a commonplace name on a contest that took place in so exotic a setting. Wingfield coined *sphairistike*, from the Greek *sphaira*, or "ball," to name the outdoor sport.

Influential friends tried it and liked everything but the name. Tradition holds that it was the philosopher-statesman Arthur

Balfour who suggested scrapping the cumbersome derivative from Greek in favor of simple "lawn tennis."

History doesn't say whether Wingfield resisted this change. At any rate he accepted it, and in February, 1874, applied for a patent on his "New and Improved Court for Playing the Ancient Game of Tennis." Though he got the patent, his court design was soon simplified. Changed from an hourglass-shaped central court with alcoves at the sides into a simple rectangle, the modified court (or "lawn") spread across the world—without bringing royalties to the man who invented its more complex predecessor.

BASEBALL

At least as early as the fourteenth century, a few dashing young European sports played club-ball, a diversion that involved swatting a ball with a club. Club-ball gave rise to a variant that some players called "rounders" because it was necessary to run around a set of safety zones or "bases" in order to score.

Rounders was played in France, England, and America, but never became widely popular.

Sometime during the 1830's Colonel Abner Doubleday of Cooperstown, New York, made a number of modifications in rounders and called the new sport "baseball." To add zest to competition, Doubleday enlarged the stick or "stump" commonly used in rounders and by that one change made it possible for players to knock balls much greater distances.

American traditions that credit Doubleday (who was later to become a general in the Union Army) with having invented what he called "base ball" without borrowing from older kinds of competition must be taken with considerably more than a grain of salt.

What Doubleday did was to take an unstructured and almost informal sport (with no fixed number of players) and devise workable rules plus some equipment that added to the drama of the sport. Alexander Joy Cartwright, a charter member of the famous Knickerbocker Club of New York, is responsible for establishing a diamond-shaped pattern of bases and for fixing the distance between bases at precisely ninety feet.

BIG LEAGUES

All early associations of baseball teams formed what would now be called "minor leagues." Adequate financing plus stadiums in which to seat large crowds were basic to big-league ball. The first big league, the National, was formed on February 2, 1876. Eight clubs were involved: Boston, Chicago, Cincinnati, Hartford, Louisville, New York, Philadelphia, and St. Louis.

Another quarter century passed before a rival league of approximately comparable strength was formed. The American League organized on January 29, 1900. Again eight clubs were involved: Buffalo, Chicago, Cleveland, Detroit, Indianapolis, Kansas City, Milwaukee, and Minneapolis.

Since only Chicago was included in both the National and the American League, the windy city has no authentic challenger for title of "home base of big-league baseball."

WORLD SERIES

An early cynic, who probably struck out when he stepped up to bat for some bush-league team, made the stinging observation that "in baseball, there are no ordinary events; everything is on a grand scale."

He may have been talking about the first official World's Championship Series. Played in 1884, it involved the rival teams of Providence, Rhode Island, and New York City (the Metropolitans). Providence won three games straight and bragged about holding the world title.

Real history was made in 1903. That year Barney Dreyfuss of the Pittsburgh Pirates wrote Henry Killilea of the Boston Red Sox proposing that "the time has come for the National and American Leagues to organize a World Series."

109

After meeting several times the two men drew up plans for a seven-game series: three to be played in Boston and four in Pittsburgh. Later the agreement was modified to stipulate that the winner of the first five games out of nine should be named World Champions.

Boston won in October, 1903, playing to a total gate of about 100,000 persons who paid an average of fifty cents each to see the Red Sox claim the first crown as World Champions —without the involvement of any team outside the United States.

PROFESSIONAL ATHLETES

Long considered the national game of England, cricket had so many adherents that authorities once considered it a nuisance. King Edward IV issued a 1477 edict forbidding his subjects to play the game because it interfered with the practice of archery.

Kings and ordinances notwithstanding, cricket flourished to such an extent that a few country clubs were formed before the end of the eighteenth century. Laborers and artisans, especially in Sussex and Kent, were as enthusiastic about it as were gentry.

More than any earlier sport, cricket lent itself to matches between different towns and villages. Later, numerous counties sponsored teams.

Once the sport became big enough to require players to travel considerable distances and consequently to miss time from work, paying them for taking part in contests seemed an obvious step. Early "players," or cricket professionals, are believed to have been the first pro athletes in the modern sense of the term.

Amateurs soon reacted by placing strict bans upon participation in their games by pros. One of the most sensational results of this dichotomy in sports occurred when Jim Thorpe was forced to give up the medals he had won at the 1912 Olympics because he had played semipro baseball.

FIVE-HUNDRED-MILE RACE

The length of early auto races varied widely. A few races that attracted especially large crowds of spectators were arbitrarily set at five hundred miles, a distance judged great enough to test the stamina of both cars and drivers.

Promoters of the now famous Indianapolis Speedway debated alternatives and decided to build a two-and-a-half-mile oval course—this length being determined by the fact that two hundred laps involved precisely five hundred miles.

Since May 30 (Memorial Day) was a major holiday in former Union territory, this date was chosen for the big race. The first five-hundred-mile race was held on Memorial Day in 1911 before a "vast crowd" of about 85,000 spectators. Forty-four cars entered the race, and thirty-eight of them crossed the finish line.

Ray Harroun, age twenty-nine, received the checkered flag after nearly seven hours at an average speed of 74.7 mph. His sixteen-cylinder Marmon "Wasp" was the talk of the country. The impact of the Indianapolis race was so great that it came to be called simply "the 500." With the current surge of interest in auto racing bringing racing to prominence as the second largest spectator sport in the United States, many races are shorter or longer than five hundred miles.

The worldwide influence of the Speedway, which was operated for a time by Eddie Rickenbacker, elevated the five hundred-mile track to such importance that this arbitrary distance is still considered ideal by major racing promoters in the United States.

VOLLEY BALL

William G. Morgan, physical director of the Holyoke, Massachusetts, YMCA, was keenly aware of the fact that many of his patrons liked basketball. This game, he felt, wasn't quite suited for business and professional men who merely wanted a workout.

Morgan experimented with ways of tossing a basketball bladder over a rope and devised a kind of contest he called mintonette. Soon after the first game was played in 1895, contestants suggested that a net be used instead of a rope. With this change and with a leather ball substituted for the light bladder first tried, the rather pompous name devised by the originator was dropped in favor of volley ball.

Just fifteen years after this sport was launched YMCA physical directors throughout the nation agreed on standard rules governing play.

BULLFIGHTING

Corrida de toros, or "a running of bulls," had its beginning as a religious ceremony. Though practiced in nearly all Mediterranean lands, it was not limited to them. Similar rites sprang up spontaneously in the Orient—notably China and Korea.

Fertility of the bull was vital to the welfare of ancients who depended largely upon cattle for necessities of life. This almost inevitably led to various types of bull-worship, of which the cults centered in Egypt are best known. The Hebrews who lived as slaves in that land learned the veneration of bulls from their masters. They later provoked the wrath of Jehovah by giving their golden ornaments to enable Aaron to fashion a "golden calf" during their wandering in the desert.

In the ancient rites dedicated to Mithras, god of light and

112

truth, the sacrificial slaughter of a bull was a central aspect of worship. The blood of the slain animal was applied to the bodies of worshipers—or drunk by them.

Gradually transformed from a mystical rite into a popular entertainment, the bullfight retains its life-or-death aspect. Some persons who go regularly to the arena say that the bloodiest of modern sports "is like a giant bath for the cleansing of man's soul." Tourists who decide to take in a fight for a lark lack the subtle cultural influences unconsciously absorbed by persons who grow up in bullfighting countries, and often become ill.

In the ancient pagan ceremonies from which the modern sport evolved, the bull always lost; not so today. One noted animal named Miuras killed seven matadors, including the legendary Manolete.

RODEO

The rodeo, as presently conducted, is youthful by comparison with other vigorous sports. The roots of present-day competitions go back to antiquity, however.

Wherever men have handled large domestic animals, skill in managing them has been regarded as a much-admired he-man trait. Ancient Greeks are known to have conducted public contests that featured such exploits as riding bucking horses and steers, wrestling animals to the ground, and the like.

As a generalization subject to conspicuous exceptions, rough outdoor sports tend to develop after a hazardous occupation has passed its zenith. Woodsmen experimented with logrolling in pioneer days, but celebrations centering in logrolling contests are modern.

Much the same thing happened on the open range. Skills that were once essential to the life of a cowboy became less important as fences were built and ranches began to be conducted in businesslike fashion. Activities that once were considered work became regarded as recreation.

No formal rodeo competion of modern style was held prior to 1888. That year, cowpokes met in competition at the Prescott, Arizona racetrack. Juan Leivas emerged as "world champion at roping and tying steers." Spreading throughout the West and then moving into eastern regions where bulldogging never was practiced as a way of making a living, the rodeo became a national and then an international spectator sport.

FOOTBALL

Games in which contestants moved balls principally or exclusively by kicking have been played since antiquity. Dozens or even hundreds of variants have been tried, and few cultures have failed to devise or adopt some such game.

An English schoolboy, William Webb Ellis, changed the history of sport with a single play. During a game at Rugby school, Ellis grabbed the ball and hugging it in his arms ran to the finish line. A stone tablet erected at his alma mater reports that "Webb thus originated the distinctive feature of the Rugby game, A.D. 1823."

Carrying the ball had been prohibited under rules previously observed.

The new sport of Rugby practically invited innovations in both offensive and defensive play. Many of the changes made by Americans were too radical for the British. As a result, American football came to be clearly distinguished from Rugby, from which it is descended.

In 1869, five years before the first international Rugby contest was held at Cambridge, Massachsetts, the football players

114

of Princeton challenged their rivals at Rutgers to a friendly game. Played at New Brunswick, New Jersey, on November 6, 1869, by teams that consisted of twenty-five men, this first intercollegiate match helped propel football into first place among U.S. college sports.

OLYMPIC GAMES

Late in the nineteenth century a number of European sports enthusiasts and a few historians conceived the idea of reviving the ancient games that the Greeks had called the Olympics. There was but one logical place to hold an international meet bringing together the finest athletes in the world. That place was Athens, Greece, where the last Olympic victor had been crowned about fifteen hundred years earlier.

Several European nations became seriously interested in the idea, but it didn't appeal to many Americans. No corporation or wealthy individual considered the project important enough to warrant paying the way for Yankees to compete. As a result, the first U.S. Olympic team was made up of just ten men—who paid their own passage.

Runners dominated the U.S. group, which also included one pole vaulter, one shot-putter, and one hurdler.

Sailing on the tramp steamer *Fulda*, bound for Naples, Italy, they left New York on March 20, 1896. Debarking on April 1, they learned that the competition would start on the sixth, twelve days earlier than they had thought. Another tramp steamer and an overnight train got them to Athens just an hour before competition began.

James Connolly, who was listed as a runner, took top honors in the first contest (hop, skip, and hop) to become the first Olympic winner to be crowned in fifteen centuries. He and his teammates won nine out of the twelve track events and created such a furor that wealthy Americans got behind the Olympic Games, and the revival proved to be a permanent one.

Music

"THE BALLAD OF JOHN HENRY"

After the Civil War, railroad owners began to introduce machinery to perform work formerly done only by men. Resentment of the mechanical competitors was so keen that some workmen deliberately destroyed equipment. Others tried to show that the machine's work was inferior to their own.

Taking the latter course was a "steel driver," or drill operator who used sledge hammers. A muscular black, John Henry drove steel in the Big Bend tunnel on the Chesapeake & Ohio Railroad near White Sulphur Springs, West Virginia, in 1870. His foreman found the progress on the job too slow and brought in a newfangled steam-driven piston drill.

The exact details have been obscured by the legends that were inspired, but there is little doubt that John Henry actually did propose a contest: man against machine. Tradition says that his foreman offered him one hundred dollars if he could beat the machine.

Using sheepnose hammers of ten pounds weight with switch handles four feet long, John Henry drove with both hands in rhythmic alternation from right to left. In a thirty-five-minute contest, say oral traditions, John Henry drove his drill through fourteen feet of hard rock—while the steam-driven rig cut through only nine feet. He collected his $100, was the hero of the railroad camp for a few hours, then died of a heart attack during the night.

"The Ballad of John Henry" has many versions whose details sometimes differ; all versions rest on the actual exploits of "a steel-driving man."

"YANKEE DOODLE"

The first patriotic song to achieve national popularity in the United States was written not by a colonist, but by a British physician, who deliberately made fun of "the homely clad colonials" in his verses.

Dr. Richard Shuckburg was regimental surgeon under the direct command of General Braddock. While stationed at Fort Crailo in Albany, New York, the sophisticated officer amused himself by writing verses that mocked trappers, tradesmen, and townsfolk.

Set to a traditional English folk tune, the song was called "Yankee Doodle." Youngsters hearing it for the first time are often puzzled because the central character "put a feather in his cap and called it 'macaroni.'" Dr. Shuckburg wasn't referring to the familiar food but to a variety of English dandy or fop whose vernacular title probably sprang from the noted Macaroni Club (whose members preferred foreign delicacies).

By using a feather to imagine himself a Macaroni, the Yankee was making a fool of himself.

Derisive though it was, the song caught the imagination of colonists and they adopted it as their own. Victorious rebels triumphantly played "Yankee Doodle" at Yorktown during the formal surrender of General Cornwallis, thus effectively turning the tables on the British writer who had considered all colonists to be country bumpkins.

"BATTLE HYMN OF THE REPUBLIC"

First published in the *Atlantic Monthly* in February, 1862, the "Battle Hymn of the Republic" is one of the most influential hymns ever written. Many military historians concur in the judgment that the hymn did more to build Union morale during the Civil War than any other single factor.

Yet it would never have been written had not the camp meeting been a major religious influence in the South.

Worshipers who laboriously sang hymns "a line at a time" used comparatively few tunes. One of their favorites, imported from England, was so stirring that several sets of words were written for it.

It was this camp-meeting melody that provided the musical background for "John Brown's Body."

After reviewing Union troops in a dress parade outside Washington, Julia Ward Howe lay awake most of the night. She had heard "John Brown's Body" over and over. Though the melody stirred her mightily, she thought little of the words.

At a hotel in the nation's capital, Mrs. Howe got out of bed and wrote new words to fit the tune to which "John Brown's Body" was sung. That is how an English melody transplanted to the U.S. South inspired "the song that won the Civil War."

NATIONAL ANTHEM

Most Americans know that "The Star-Spangled Banner" grew out of a military engagement. Millions who have visited the Smithsonian Institution have been surprised at the enormous size of the flag that attorney Francis Scott Key saw by gunfire.

Few persons realize, though, that the song was in existence for 117 years before it became the national anthem.

Almost from the time it was written in 1814, patriots used it in rallies and ceremonies. No other song evoked quite the same response. Yet its place of honor was wholly unofficial—a matter of custom.

Herbert Hoover was the president who played the final scene

in the drama leading to formal recognition of the song's place in American life. Congress passed an act designating "The Star-Spangled Banner" to be "the national anthem of the United States of America," and President Hoover made it official with a stroke of the pen on March 3, 1931.

RECORDING BY A STAR

Long after Thomas Edison's phonograph had proved its merit, big-name musicians and singers shunned the device. Early commerical records were generally of poor quality and were produced in small quantity. No one connected with the world of music had the slightest idea that records would ever develop into a huge business enterprise.

Officials of the Gramophone Company were certain that a market existed. In order to reach it, however, they had to offer the public a superior product—and a well-known name. After a series of negotiations they reached agreement with Enrico Caruso.

For a fee of five hundred dollars, the world-famous singer recorded a series of ten arias. He sang in a "studio" improvised from a room in the Hotel di Milano in Milan, Italy. In spite of makeshift working arrangements, the records cut on March 18, 1902, proved to be the first completely satisfactory set ever made.

With Caruso's name as sales bait, the Gramophone Com-

119

pany recovered its investment many times over—and the practice of releasing recordings by stars was born.

"AMERICA"

Schoolchildren of Boston, Massachusetts, assembled for a Fourth of July celebration in 1832. Their meeting, held in Park Street Baptist Church, was to be a major event of the season.

As "a special treat" the boys and girls were given an opportunity to sing a new patriotic hymn written by the church's pastor, Dr. Samuel Francis Smith.

Smith was gifted with words but lacked the ability to write a suitable tune. So he turned to the British composition "God Save the King," and borrowed it for the song to celebrate independence from the king. A poem of praise to America, set to the tune of "God Save the King," was completed in half an hour.

To the surprise of everyone, Smith most of all, the song he entitled "America" brought an ovation. Its popularity quickly spread throughout the nation, and the hastily scribbled manuscript became so prized that it was given a place of honor in the Harvard University museum.

"GOD BLESS AMERICA!"

Russian-born Israel Baline Berlin came to the United States in 1893 as a child of five. Educated in the public schools of New York, he was a far more ardent patriot than many persons born on American soil.

During World War I this man—who had changed his name to Irving Berlin—wrote the score for the soldier show *Yip Yip Yaphank*. Before the production went on stage, he deleted from it a number that he had titled "God Bless America."

Twenty-two years later, in 1939, Kate Smith made a feverish search for a new patriotic song to use in her Armistice Day broadcast. She found the long neglected piece by a naturalized citizen and sang it on November 11. Heard by the American public for the first time that day, it was an instant success. It has frequently been suggested as a replacement for the national anthem, which is so hard to sing.

Delighted and deeply moved, Irving Berlin insisted that though he had written the song "it belongs to the nation." He refused to accept any royalties and turned over the earnings from "God Bless America!" to the Boy Scouts and Girl Scouts of America.

"MEET ME IN ST. LOUIS"

Long before cities and states began establishing tourist bureaus to lure visitors and their dollars, civic leaders in St. Louis planned a lavish exposition. Timed to coincide with the centennial of the Louisiana Purchase, it involved an unprecedented outlay of money.

Clearly, everything possible had to be done in order to arouse national interest in the exposition. The song-writing team of Andrew Sterling and Kerry Mills attacked the problem and came up with a catchy tune and a vivid set of words. By January, 1905, people all over America were singing and humming "Meet me in St. Louis, Louis, meet me at the Fair," and were flocking to the river city in such numbers that the success of the "fair" launched the modern wave of international expositions.

"DIXIE"

Daniel Decatur Emmett, a native of Ohio, drifted to New York and became a member of the city's growing colony of musicians and actors. Brant's Minstrels, who performed at 472 Broadway, decided they needed "a plantation song and dance" for their show. Emmett was commissioned to write the music and compose the melody.

His finished product, "I Wish I Was in Dixie's Land," had its public debut in Mechanics Hall, New York City, on

121

April 4, 1859. Manhattan's Firth Pond & Co. published it.

On a visit to Alabama the writer-composer met one of America's foremost musicians. Herman F. Arnold, a recent immigrant from Germany, was conductor of the finest orchestra in the region. He heard Emmett's new song, liked it so well that he used the tune to serenade and win his bride, an aristocratic belle of Montgomery, Alabama, named Victoria Luciana.

It was Herman Arnold who planned and led the music for the inauguration of Jefferson Davis as first president of the Confederacy. At the height of the ceremony on February 18, 1861, Arnold and his musicians burst forth with "Dixie."

And so an Ohio Yankee, a New York publisher, and an immigrant from Germany gave the South the song that most persons consider a product of antebellum plantation life.

"LA CUCARACHA"

Long before marijuana surged to prominence in the United States it was widely used in other cultures. Many observers noted the effects of the weed, known to botanists as *cannabis*, upon humans who used it. Perhaps it was some village jokester who first quipped that it would be very funny to see an insect who had become addicted to marijuana. Again, it may have been a sponstaneous idea that emerged in some obscure barroom where patrons used both marijuana and alcohol.

Capitalizing upon the idea, a Spanish composer who knew little about the ways of insects (who actually refuse to eat or even to pollinate cannabis) wrote a song about a cockroach hooked on marijuana. Using the term for "cockroach" in his native language, he called the dashing piece simply "La Cucaracha."

CROONING

Within a year after Radio Station KDKA in Pittsburgh, Pennsylvania, launched the first scheduled broadcasting service late in 1920, thousands of persons remained glued to their sets during the hours when there was something to hear. Reception was poor, for equipment was extremely clumsy by modern standards.

Broadcasters had their technical problems, too. One of the most serious of these grew out of the limitations of the microphones of that day. Since mikes couldn't take loud volume, the voices of most persons who tried to sing were hopelessly distorted.

In October, 1921, Miss Vaughn De Leath licked the technical problem. Instead of singing in the customary manner, she tried a low-volume style that she called "crooning."

Though microphones were soon improved so that they could take greater volumes of sound, the impact of radio had made the new method of singing a national fad. Recognizing this trend, in 1929 the National Broadcasting Company launched a series of weekly programs featuring a saxophone player from Maine. During the ten years that his "Connecticut Yankees" accompanied him, Rudy Vallee became the all-time king of "sweet and low" singers.

PHONOGRAPH—AND THE RECORD

About the middle of August in 1877, Thomas Edison completed work on a crude model of a "talking machine." Together with terse notes about its principles he turned it over to an assistant, John Kreusi, to produce a finished working model. Like most of the men who worked for Edison, Kreusi was paid on a piecework basis. Before he started on this job he knew he would receive eighteen dollars for it.

Kreusi had muttered that he didn't think the machine would work, and offered to bet Edison two dollars that his boss was wrong.

Four months later, Kreusi's assignment was completed. In order to test the new machine, Edison sent young George Atwood down the street to find "the lady who plays the piano." Atwood came back with Miss Harriet Hadden, who sat down at the keyboard and played the melody cut into the world's first phonograph record.

On November 21, Edison triumphantly reported success with his talking machine—then reminded Kreusi of their bet and collected two dollars from his assistant.

George Atwood, who later became an electrical engineer with Western Electric and helped to develop the dial telephone system, became increasingly interested in Harriet Hadden. His role in the successful test of the phonograph and production of the first record brought him no financial reward —but "the lady who plays the piano" became Mrs. George Atwood.

"ALOHA OE"

Many heads of state, both male and female, have tried their hands at writing poetry and songs. Only one sovereign of a nation has succeeded in producing music that has become truly international in its appeal. That person was Mrs. Lydia Dominis, the sister of King Kalakaua who succeeded him to the throne.

Fellow Hawaiians preferred to call her Liliuokalani. She put many native melodies into writing, and adapted and transformed others. Among them was an almost hypnotic song that transcended speech barriers in a unique fashion.

"Aloha Oe" was already popular in Hawaii before Liliuokalani assumed the reins of government as regent while her brother made an around-the-world tour in 1881. Frequently sung at state occasions during the period that Queen Liliuokalani ruled Hawaii, the song was taken back home by visiting diplomats and won the hearts of the people of the world.

"I'LL TAKE YOU HOME AGAIN, KATHLEEN"

Tom Westendorf was desperate. His wife, mourning the loss of their son, appeared to be on the verge of a breakdown.

124

Their family doctor had suggested a trip to Kathy's home in New York, but they didn't have the money to go.

"Hang on a little longer, and things will change," he promised his wife. Songs that he had submitted to a Cincinnati publisher were being returned promptly, but Tom pretended that a big contract was in the offing.

Cheered by the prospect of paying her mother a visit, Kathy grew better. But the cost of a trip to New York remained prohibitive.

Tom had made up a little song—nothing so important as his serious compositions, of course—about taking his wife on that all-important visit. Sometimes he hummed the words as he worked on projects that might finance the trip.

Unable to sleep one night, he decided to put the familiar words and tune of the household song upon paper. Since he knew them by heart he worked rapidly, changing an occasional word here and a note there.

"I'll Take You Home Again, Kathleen" was an instant hit and has remained a perennial favorite. Many persons who treasure it regard it as an old Irish song—not knowing that it was written in Virginia by a man whose goal was to return to the Empire State.

"HAIL TO THE CHIEF!"

During his first term as president, James Madison enjoyed popularity rarely if ever equalled by a chief executive. An era of "good feeling" swept the nation with such impact that in the election of 1820 Monroe received all but one of the 232 votes cast by members of the Electoral College. (William Plumer of New Hampshire voted for John Quincy Admas—not because he was opposed to Monroe, but because he felt Washington should be the only man to be elected by a unanimous vote.)

Monroe's second inauguration was set for Monday, March 5, 1821. Against all precedent, the men in charge of planning the ceremony decided that it would be held outdoors. As a special salute to "the most popular American" they set out to find a new and vivid musical composition that could be introduced during the inauguration.

U.S. composers and performers failed to produce anything judged suitable. So the talent scouts fanned out over Europe and found what they wanted in a most unlikely place. A few months earlier some words of Sir Walter Scott's narrative poem "Lady of the Lake" had been set to music by James Sanderson and E. Rilley.

Entitled "Hail to the Chief!" the composition really did serve as a high point of the inaugural ceremonies, causing it to be associated with the prestige of the President of the United States rather than the might of a Scottish chieftain.

"SWEET ADELINE"

Operatic coloratura soprano Adelina Patti, born in Madrid in 1843, reigned for many years as one of the queens of international opera. During the latter part of the century, many connoisseurs agreed that it was a waste of time to hear any other singer in the roles of Linda, Norina, Lucia, Violetta, and Zerlina.

Still vigorous and in good voice at age sixty, she appeared in New York for a special engagement. Owners of the theater where she sang abandoned all other methods of advertising and simply spelled out on the marquee in huge letters the announcement: ADELINA PATTI.

Henry Armstrong and Richard Gerard, a writer-composer team with a feel for the barber-shop constituency, passed the theater one day and saw the name of the great operatic singer. From this inspiration they wrote "Sweet Adeline," which was sung in New York City for the first time on December 27, 1903—and which has been sung by someone, somewhere, practically every hour of every day since.

"DEAR FRIENDS AND GENTLE HEARTS"

During the period before the Civil War no native-born author-composer was more widely acclaimed than Stephen Foster. Many of his best-loved works were issued by the New York firm of Firth, Pond & Co.

In 1854 his publishers gleefully announced his total sales to date: "Old Folks at Home," more than 130,000 copies; "My Old Kentucky Home," 90,000; "Massa's in De Cold, Cold Ground," 74,000; and "Old Dog Tray," 48,000.

His success failed to bring tranquillity to Foster's restless heart. For a considerable period he actually found himself unable to do creative work.

Late in 1863 or early in 1864 he started work on a new song. Written in his own hand on a little slip of paper, the manuscript of "Dear Friends and Gentle Hearts" was found in his pocket along with all his worldly goods—thirty-five cents—when he passed out in his hotel room. Three days later, on January 13, he died in Bellevue Hospital without knowing that the song he wrote from the pit of despair was destined to become immortal.

Business and Industry

FLEA MARKET

Late in the last century French *chiffonniers* (rag pickers) who daily combed the trash cans of Paris began accumulating so much saleable merchandise that a few of them opened little shops near the northern walls of the city. This nucleus attracted other beginning and small-time dealers in used, old, and unusual items. English bargain-hunters who prowled through the region complained that the merchants were so infested with vermin that the only proper name for the conglomeration of stalls was the Flea Market.

Now consisting of more than three thousand individual business establishments that offer commodities ranging from secondhand hardware to German helmets, and from false teeth to oriental rugs, the Paris Flea Market sprawls over many acres near the Porte de Clignancourt.

Visitors to the exotic city who came away clutching "fantastic bargains" such as nineteenth-century dolls and Baccarat crystal (somewhat chipped) proudly exhibited their purchases when they got home. Americans caught the general idea, and flea markets were opened in many major cities and rapidly spread into numerous towns in the United States.

MOTELS

The growing traffic on the state's expanding road system gave an idea to Californian Arthur S. Heineman. In 1925 he

128

designed and built near the highway at San Luis Obispo a facility that offered motorists a place to sleep—with parking places only a few steps away from the doorways.

One story says that the architect planned to call his lodging place "Milestone Motor Hotel." Finding that this name required too large a sign, he abbreviated it to Milestone Mo-Tel.

Though there is no documentary evidence behind this account, the American Automobile Association vouches for the fact that Heineman's roadside establishment did bear the hyphenated name Mo-Tel.

A series of cabins was arranged around a court behind a main building that housed the lounge, dining room, and business office. Each cabin had an attached garage.

Motorists liked the novel arrangement, but insisted on modifying the name to *motel*. That term was registered with the State of California, but since it designated a form of service rather than a unique product it never gained the status of a trademark.

Though a few other "motor hotels" were built by 1930, most families who traveled by car in that era tented in auto camps or rented rooms (at rates ranging from fifty cents to one dollar in residences that doubled as "tourist homes"). The real boom in motel building in the United States came after World War II.

FREE ROAD MAPS

William Akin, head of a small advertising agency in Pittsburgh, was driving his 1912 Chalmers along Baum Boulevard one day in 1914. An ardent motorist, he had an idea that giveaway maps would be ideal advertising pieces for oil companies.

He may have used one or more maps published by the American Automobile Association. The first AAA map was issued about 1905 and covered Staten Island, New York. All copies of it have disappeared, however, and even the exhaustive collection in the AAA library includes no map earlier than 1911. Relatively small numbers were printed and motorists prized these maps highly.

Akin suggested to Gulf Refining Company that free maps would prove excellent lures with which to woo customers. Manager Gale Nutty decided to test their sales impact, and so mailed free maps to ten thousand auto owners. Later he produced monthly maps showing drivers how to reach points of interest within twenty-five miles of Pittsburgh. By 1915, Gulf was producing a yearly total of three hundred thousand maps covering various northeastern states.

Other oil companies borrowed the idea and produced their own maps; free distribution became a standard practice.

Today, about 200 million free maps are passed out annually to U.S. motorists. With costs rising, many companies would like to abandon the practice of giving away maps—but when they have tried, customer reaction has been so strong that sales managers have concluded that free maps are here to stay.

EIGHT-HOUR DAY

Soon after the Civil War a few idealists denounced then prevalent standards calling for workweeks of sixty to seventy-two hours during six days. A day should be equally divided between work, sleep, and leisure, propagandists argued.

Most employers scoffed at such nonsense, and only a few workmen publicly backed the idea of dividing the day into equal thirds. Endorsement of the eight-hour day came from the Machinists and Blacksmiths Union in 1860; six years later, at its first annual congress, the National Labor Union came out in favor of the idea.

President Andrew Johnson startled everyone, even the members of Congress who had voted for the act, when he signed a bill providing that "eight hours shall constitute a day's work for all laborers, workmen, and mechanics who may be employed by or on behalf of the Government of the United States."

Signed on June 25, 1868, this statute was conspicuous for its omission of any reference to white-collar workers. It wasn't until 1912 that the U.S. government adopted the eight-hour day for all its employees.

The eight-hour day was grudgingly accepted by business

and industry, and the workweek was shortened to five and a half days and then to five. The principle of "one-third of a day for work" is now being challenged from a new direction. As an incentive for longer weekends, some industries are experimenting with nine- and even ten-hour workdays. Early reports show that four "long days" are as fruitful as five eight-hour days.

NEW YORK STOCK EXCHANGE

Until the War of Independence, stockbrokers operating in the New World were controlled by parent firms in London. The freedom from restraint granted by the war soon led to confusion and then to chaos. Dealers in stocks and bonds competed for business by dropping their commissions and fees to points a fraction below those of leading firms.

Something had to be done. As a protective measure to eliminate fee-cutting, twenty-four brokers met on May 17, 1792, and signed a formal agreement. Essentially a protective league, the organization known as the New York Stock Exchange was revamped in 1817 along lines that led it to become the world's biggest center for buying and selling stocks and securities.

SKYSCRAPER

Until the 1880's most architects and builders insisted that it was impossible to erect a structure more than six or seven

131

stories in height. Anything taller than that, said experts, would collapse under its own weight.

Major William Le Baron Jenney disagreed. He persuaded officials of New York's Home Insurance Company that he could go higher and that a towering building would give the company priceless free publicity.

Jenney designed a steel-skeleton building of ten stories in such fashion that the marble walls did not bear the weight of the structure. Instead, even the marble was supported by a steel frame.

Erected at the corner of La Salle and Adams Street in Chicago and completed in the fall of 1885, the structure proved so strong that two additional stories were added to it later. Truly a marvel of engineering, and for years one of the great sights in America, this fantastic structure towered so far above the streets of the city that awed visitors called it "the skyscraper." Later, the title became attached to buildings so tall that Major Jenney's masterpiece was made to seem puny.

CHAIN STORE

Partly because he worked hard, partly because his customers liked him, New York merchant George Huntington Hartford soon attracted a good clientele for the hide and leather business he opened in 1857. It occurred to him, though, that a small sideline would add to his profits. What commodity would a purchaser of hides or leather be likely to pick up on impulse?

No doubt about it, Hartford concluded, the ideal product was tea. He added this to his line of merchandise in 1859 and found that his profits did increase substantially.

Tea proved so profitable that he elevated it to first place, developed a plan for central purchasing and packaging while retailing through a group or "chain" of outlets. In 1869 Hartford reorganized his firm as the Great Atlantic and Pacific Tea Company.

His methods proved so efficient and profitable that a host of imitators launched other chain stores. Several of them spread much faster than Hartford's company—which despite its name didn't open its first Pacific coast store until 1930.

FIVE-CENT STORE

After a boyhood on the farm Frank Winfield Woolworth entered business at age nineteen. He soon became impatient with his work as a clerk and decided to open his own store. No ordinary store, it would offer no mechandise selling for more than ten cents.

Hoping to attract a large number of customers, Woolworth priced the bulk of his merchandise at five cents and advertised the opening of his Five-Cent Store in Utica, New York, early in 1879. Unlike the "five-cent table" he had operated earlier at the Watertown, New York, county fair the store attracted little interest and few customers. Some weeks, the total sales were as low as $2.50.

Convinced that he had a good idea but a bad location, Woolworth moved to Lancaster, Pennsylvania, after just four months. Here his innovation in merchandising proved a big success. Eventually he built a nationwide chain of stores, and attracted several highly successful competitors.

As merchandising methods and the economy changed, young Woolworth's innovation went through a unique series of modifications in title. His original "five-cent store" gave birth to the "five and ten," was soon transformed into the "dime store," and now is fast giving way to the "dollar store." In a bona fide dollar store, no item is priced above one dollar—but at the check-out stands of dime stores it isn't unusual to see cashiers ring up charges of $3.99, $5.95, or even $9.98.

CAFETERIA

The prosperity of the Gay Nineties proved a mixed blessing to operators of eating establishments. Patrons had more money to spend, but waiters were increasingly independent. Some of them flatly refused to work unless they received wages that seemed ridiculously high.

Chicago businessman Ernest Kimball had an inspiration. Why not eliminate the cost and nuisance of waiters, let patrons serve themselves, and use part of the money saved to cut prices below the competition?

Kimball opened his self-service eating establishment in 1895. It worked so well that four years later he moved it to the basement of the New York Life Building, where it was visited by so many out-of-town guests that the cafeteria concept quickly fanned out and spread across America.

SUPERMARKET

Virginia-born Clarence Saunders entered the grocery business directly from the farm. Not being trained in the way stores had to be operated, he chafed at the inertia he sensed in the field.

In 1916 he launched a small chain of groceries designed to be operated with a minimum amount of labor. Most goods were placed on shelves where customers could choose what they wanted and take their selections to a cashier.

Saunders called these self-service groceries Piggily-Wiggily stores. He kept prices low and used flamboyant advertising programs. On the opening day of a new store each redheaded woman who made a purchase was handed a bouquet of roses; a brass band played at the entrance all day; and colored balloons floated above the crowds.

Four years after he began using these tactics keyed to a radical new system of merchandising, Saunders had 2,660 stores in operation. Competing chains sprang up; some of them branched out into merchandise other than groceries. By 1930, just fourteen years after the Piggily-Wiggily innovations began, self-service groceries had blossomed into supermarkets with thousands of items on their shelves and only a handful of persons working in them.

LABOR STRIKE

England's hatmakers, long organized into a guild, became increasingly dissatisfied with their wages and working conditions after Charles Townshend was made Chancellor of the Exchequer in 1766. It didn't help when Edmund Burke publicly labeled him "a tessellated pavement without cement."

Matters went from bad to worse; on May 9, 1768, the makers of hats laid down their tools and said they would work no more until their pay was raised. From the sailor's practice of striking sail when port was reached and their work was finished, the collective action of the hatters was derided as a "strike."

Both the name and the pattern of resistance spread rapidly. Philadelphia printers struck in 1786—and won a wage increase of six dollars per week. British colliers, who struck seven years later, were not so fortunate; the mine owners discharged them and put new crews to work. As late as 1810, public opinion was heavily weighted against attempted coercion by means of strikes. That year, New York courts heard charges that members of the Journeymen Cordwainers (a shoemakers' union) had "conspired to call a strike." Found guilty, the union was ordered to pay court costs and each member had to forfeit one dollar.

Now infinitely more complex than workers merely laying down their tools and refusing to work, the strike has developed from its obscure beginnings to become one of the major forces affecting not simply industry, but all phases of modern society.

NEWSPAPER ADVERTISEMENTS

Printed advertisements were in circulation soon after the pioneer English printer, William Caxton, began making innovations in the art. But the advertisements issued by Caxton and his successors were in the form of small cards that announced the availability of goods and services; larger pieces called handbills appeared a bit later.

English civil wars in the seventeenth century created a climate favorable to the development of newspapers, but early papers depended entirely upon the sale of copies for revenue.

Booksellers are believed to have been the first businessmen to seize upon the idea of buying space in newspapers in order to advertise their wares. One of the earliest paid notices that has been preserved appeared in London, in number 13 of the paper bearing the formidable title *Perfect Occurrences of Every Daie Journall in Parliament and other Moderate Intelligence.*

A volume that capitalized upon religious differences of the day, printed and published for Joseph Hunscot and Charles Calvert and sold at both the Stationers' Hall and the Golden Fleece Pub, evoked that notable newspaper ad. History doesn't record the number of books sold as a result of it, but the idea caught on and merchants began using newspaper advertisements as their prime channel of communication with potential customers.

BOOK PUBLISHING

Johann Gutenberg, who is generally credited with having developed the art of printing with movable type, had so little capital that he was forced to use his equipment as security for borrowed money.

Johann Fust, a prosperous financier in Mainz, advanced eight hundred guilders to Gutenberg to help him get a start. Two years later he put up an equal sum and became a full partner of the man who was sure he would succeed in producing printed Bibles in quantity.

Five years passed without completion of the project, so Fust demanded his money. Principal plus compound interest ran the debt up to what was then a considerable sum—about 2,025 guilders.

Gutenberg couldn't begin to pay that amount. He surrendered his equipment plus his unfinished Bibles. His creditor then employed Peter Schoeffer, chief assistant to the printer, to "bring the noble task to conclusion."

Using Gutenberg's idea and fortified with quantities of nearly completed volumes, Schoeffer bound a quantity of them (variously estimated at 120 to 250) in 1456 and began selling them.

Publisher Fust, who had provided nothing except money, maintained control of the world's first firm devoted to production of printed books. Embittered and impoverished, Gutenberg, who made the whole thing possible, died in 1468 without getting any reward except personal satisfaction.

COMMERCIAL RADIO BROADCASTING

Radio pioneer Reginald A. Fessenden succeeded in broadcasting what he called "a program of voice and music" on December 24, 1906. A message was transmitted from New York to Chicago just three years later.

In spite of continuing progress by technicians and inventors, radio remained an amateur device until 1920. That year, Pittsburgh's powerful station KDKA gambled and won.

On November 2, KDKA went on the air as soon as the first election returns were available. Hour after hour, men who didn't think of themselves as announcers or commentators reported the progress of the struggle for the Presidency between Warren G. Harding and James M. Cox.

Though the broadcast was costly by standards of the day, it had comparatively few listeners. Those fortunate enough to live within range of Pittsburgh kept their earphones on hour after hour, elated at receiving up-to-the-minute news by air.

So much interest was created that the business launched by a hotly contested presidential election expanded and began live coverage of major sporting events. Governor Cox of Ohio,

137

whose defeat was reported by KDKA that momentous November in 1920, retaliated after a fashion by purchasing some radio stations of his own and adding them to the chain of newspapers he already owned.

ASSEMBLY LINE

Long ago, manufacturers and builders experimented with use of interchangeable precision-made parts. This process was employed in the manufacture of rifles that helped to win the War of Independence. Early in the nineteenth century, religious zealots who founded the community of New Harmony, Indiana, mastered all the fundamentals of the prefabricated house.

Achievements of this sort were sporadic in nature and local in influence. The principles they embodied were finally used by an industrial genius to develop mass-production.

Henry Ford launched the world's first formal assembly line on January 14, 1914. Though workmen soon began complaining that their jobs were monotonous, the procedure of assembling a car while it remained in continuous motion paid big dividends in time. Late in 1913, Ford mechanics required an average of about 12½ hours to put one car together. Before the end of January, 1914, the time for complete assembly had been cut to 93 minutes.

Once the economic feasibility of the new technique had been demonstrated, it was only a matter of time before it was being applied to the manufacture of products ranging from wood-burning kitchen stoves to the most sophisticated weapons and vehicles used by Americans in World War I.

BEST-SELLER LIST

Editors of the British trade journal *Bookman* held a conference in 1895 and concurred that something vital was lacking in the publishing scene. Everyone in the business knew what books were being published, but no one had more than a smattering of information about the success of individual titles.

As a service to their readers, editors of *Bookman* began listing "books in demand" in various cities. They didn't go about the process of sampling in scientific fashion, so their lists didn't always reflect consumer tastes accurately. Still, the idea of giving an account of best-selling titles created such interest that it has continued ever since.

Today, everyone in the publishing business knows that its appearance on a major "best-seller list" not only says something about what readers think of a book, it also has the effect of boosting sales because great numbers of persons who aren't serious readers take care to buy some best-sellers.

SERVICE STATION

Two major American cities are rival claimants to the honor of having given the world the gasoline service station, but neither city has preserved the name of the man who first went into the business.

Early motorists bought what little gasoline they used in livery stables and garages. No one then thought that liquid fuel would provide a big enough base to support a business.

Pittsburgh auto buffs say the first establishment that sold only gasoline and oil was opened for business on December 1, 1913. What's more, local tradition asserts, the amount of fuel pumped on that first day amounted to just thirty gallons.

St. Louis historians insist that the first drive-in gasoline station in the world opened there in 1905 at the corner of Theresa and Market Streets. The fuel is reliably said to have been pumped through a garden hose, but no one knows how much was retailed on the first day.

For years operators of gas stations concentrated purely on the sale of their special commodities. The growing rivalry between big national chains led to an increasing emphasis on attracting customers by means of gratis services: air, water, windshield-washing, and the like.

One of the earliest authenticated references to a service station, as distinguished from the gas station that gave birth to it, appears in Sinclair Lewis's novel *Babbit*, which was published in 1922.

TELEPHONE DIRECTORY

The solution of technological problems made the telephone a workable reality well before the establishment of elaborate systems was economically feasible. Practically all pioneer "phones" were installed for use by persons of wealth and prominence, and at first were used chiefly for urgent messages.

Since New Haven, Connecticut, was noted for its wealth and rich cultural life, telephone service grew more rapidly here than in most rival cities. Eventually there were so many people with phones in the city that hardly anyone could remember all of the numbers.

On February 21, 1878, the New Haven Telephone Company decided to give its subscribers a bonus in the form of a list of names and numbers. That pioneer telephone directory consisted of just fifty listings. From that beginning, the telephone directory grew into one of the most widely used of all information services.

DRIVE-INS

The growing popularity of motion pictures plus the increasing availability of motor cars caused an idea to take shape in the minds of two New Jersey businessmen. Families with small children would be delighted to watch the flickers from their cars, reasoned Richard M. Hollingshead, Jr., and Willis W. Smith. Besides, courting couples would welcome an opportunity for a bit of privacy along with their entertainment.

On June 6, 1933, Hollingshead and Smith opened a drive-in motion-picture theater. Their huge screen—forty by fifty feet—was the talk of the region. Rows of inclined planes permitted patrons to see the screen from each of about five hundred cars.

An instant success, the drive-in theater has spawned a host of diverse establishments that have nothing in common except their focus upon patrons who wish to do business without leaving their cars. Drive-in restaurants, drive-in banks, drive-in cleaning establishments, and drive-in churches, taken collectively, now greatly outnumber the still popular drive-in theaters.

TIMETABLE

Though most early trains had specified times at which they arrived at and departed from their stations, they were often hours—and sometimes days—behind schedule.

Officials of the Baltimore and Ohio Railroad decided that they would get more passengers if the trains ran on time and members of the general public knew when to expect them. As a venture in public relations and advertising, the B & O published on May 20, 1830, a schedule of the departures and arrivals of trains running between Baltimore and Ellicott's Mills, Maryland.

This first recorded timetable was not issued as a pocket-size folder; instead it appeared as a notice in the *Baltimore American*. Proliferation of competing railroads plus adoption of standard time (in lieu of "sun time") made it not only possible but essential that passengers be provided with time-tables. With the advent of the public bus and the commercial airline, the device that was born to inform persons when they could go to and from Ellicott's Mills became a vital ingredient in planning trips a few miles down the road or around the world.

Medicine and Health

ASPIRIN

Aspirin has no close competitor for the rank of "most widely used drug of all time." Annually, millions of tons are consumed the world around, chiefly for relief of headache, muscular pains, and discomfort associated with the common cold.

Yet pain-dulling effects that make it the number one analgesic in the pharmacopoeia were discovered by accident rather than through research aimed at this goal.

Felix Hoffmann, a young German chemist, was seeking something to relieve his father's rheumatoid arthritis. Acetylsalicylic acid $(C_9H_8O_4)$ had been known for almost half a century, but wasn't regarded as important.

Used experimentally by Hoffmann in 1898, it performed as he had hoped. Unexpectedly, it had the effect of relieving a whole spectrum of bodily pains not associated with arthritis.

Officials of the Frederich Bayer Company in Düsseldorf, Germany, realized that they had something important. Adapting native terms for the spirea plant, which yields a basic constitutent of the drug, it was marketed under the trade name of Aspirin.

Aspirin remained a proprietary drug until after World War I. In a famous decision of 1921, Judge Learned Hand ruled that the chemical (earlier seized by U.S. authorities under the Alien Property Act) was so universally known as aspirin that no manufacturer was entitled to a royalty for permission to use that name.

Every year since 1899, sales have increased; no other drug—

whether produced by concerted research or by a chance dis-covery—has had so long a record of continuous acceptance by moderns.

CARDIAC SURGERY

Today's widely varied and often dramatic operations upon the human heart are in great measure the result of self-ex-perimentation by a courageous pioneer.

Until 1929 no one had any positive "inside information" about the heart. Dr. Werner Forssmann suggested inserting a catheter into a vein and then working the instrument for-ward until it reached the vital organ. A great idea, but who would risk his life by trying it?

In the end it was Dr. Forssmann himself who pushed the catheter into the right auricle of his own heart. Findings made as a result of this pioneer experiment on the only person willing to take the risks involved brought Forssmann the Nobel Prize—and launched a new era in medicine by making cardiac surgery practicable.

MORPHINE

Working with the crude mixture that apothecaries of the era called "opium salt," German tradesman F. W. A. Sertürner extracted a drug that he considered to be relatively pure. Soon after it became available in 1805, the drug showed amazing capacity to lull sick persons to sleep. Named after the Greek god of sleep, it was called *morphine.*

Setürner made the first recorded test of the powerful com-pound upon himself, when he had a toothache. It worked so well that he continued his experiments for a considerable period. His work opened up a new field of medicine by showing the action of the first alkaloid from natural sources.

It remains a scientific mystery how the apothecary was able to use so much morphine over so long a period without becoming addicted to it.

VITAMINS

In an era when pellagra was regarded as a contagious disease Dr. Joseph Goldberger came to the conclusion that some other factor was involved. He spent the period 1913-25 hunting that "something else," and finally became convinced that nutritional deficiences cause the condition.

His fellow physicians scoffed.

In order to prove that pellagra can't be transmitted from one person to another, the doctor, who was working for the U.S. Public Health Service, ate contaminated matter from the bodies of pellagra sufferers.

He persuaded the governor of Mississippi to offer clemency to a group of prisoners on condition that they take part in a carefully controlled experiment that might cause some of them to come down with pellagra. Dividing his subjects into two groups, the fiery little physician from the ghetto of New York fed some prisoners a diet consisting largely of grits and other corn products. Meanwhile, he gave the others fresh milk and vegetables.

The dramatic results achieved at Mississippi State Prison gave conclusive evidence that pellagra is an effect of dietary deficiencies. These findings led to the discovery of the role of vitamins and the modern emphasis upon a balanced diet.

GUINEA PIG

Early explorers of South America were largely motivated by greed for gold, but found themselves intrigued by the flora and fauna of the strange continent. They brought many plants and animals back to Europe and tried to propagate them. Most such efforts failed, but one enjoyed great success.

A little rodent with hooflike nails, widely distributed in South America, quickly adapted to the climate of Europe. "Guinea," originally the name of a district on the west coast of Africa, had entered popular speech as a label for any far-off land of mystery. This title seemed just right for the South American animal. So in spite of the fact that it didn't come from Guinea and it is not a pig, the queer creature came into prominence as the guinea pig.

Its fertility, placid disposition, and small size made the guinea pig an ideal laboratory animal. Used in thousands of experiments and studies, the once insignificant creature played a key role in many major medical discoveries. Until challenged by rhesus monkeys and white rats, the odd rodent from South America was without rival for first place among laboratory animals contributing to the understanding and control of disease.

FORCEPS

Devices with which to handle hot metal were in use very soon after the close of the Stone Age. Artisans probably employed leather pads to hold hot pieces of iron prior to the time that metal implements came into vogue.

Very early, obstetricians adapted the forceps of the smith for use with mothers whose babies died before delivery. A pair of long, smooth forceps with serrated tips (widely known as "crocodile beaks") proved effective in removing foetal remains. For centuries physicians and metalworkers alike made futile efforts to perfect a "taking device" with which to help mothers who were having difficulty delivering live babies. Success was finally achieved by a refugee.

William Chamberlen (or Chambellan) had a good practice in Paris but was a Hugenot. So he fled in 1569 and settled in England. His oldest son, also a physician, may have perfected a utensil created by his father, or he may have invented it without help. Because it was kept as a family secret for more than a century, the details concerning the invention of the obstetrical forceps remain obscure.

This wonderful device for taking a baby enabled the Chamberlens to build an enormous practice, and it became one of the most talked-about mechanical inventions of the era. Pirated and copied by other physicians, forceps, one of the most jealously guarded of all medical innovations, came into general use and have undergone few basic changes since the sixteenth century.

ALCOHOL

Scientific archaeology has revealed that women have been using cosmetics for many centuries. Throughout the ancient Near East it was customary to darken the eyelids in order to increase the luster of the eyes.

A variety of substances were used as eye make-up: powdered antimony, antimony trisulphide, powdered galena or lead ore, smoke-black obtained from burnt almond shells, and even the residue from burnt frankincense. Arabs used "kohl" to designate any powder that women mixed with oil and then smeared on their eyelids. In Latin, a mixture that included kohl as an ingredient was termed *alcohol*.

Early chemists turned to this imported word as a designation for any fine powder or essence produced by sublimation or trituration. It was in this sense that flower of brimstone was sometimes called "alcohol of suphur." Essence, or spirit of wine, was for a time known as "alcohol."

Ordinary folk and then physicians and scientists used the term as a shorthand label for any variety of rectified spirits. It wasn't until comparatively modern times that research proved alcohol second only to water in importance as a solvent. As a result alcohol has found many important, even unique, roles

147

in medicine. This turn of events puts this product of fermentation exactly where it was thousands of years ago when, known by other names, the potent stuff was employed as a virtual cure-all, and as a component in more primitive medicines than any other substance.

ETHER

From the earliest times to the present, all civilizations and people have wrestled with fundamental questions: How did life begin? When was the world formed? What raw material was used in making it?

Ancient theorists, pondering the latter problem, proposed that a single substance, or "element," fills all space beyond the sphere of the moon and is a basic constitutent of the sun, stars, and planets.

This mysterious stuff, ether, was discussed in the ancient cosmological sense by English thinkers of the fifteenth century. Poets, chemists, and physicists as well as philosophers used the label almost indiscriminately.

One of the many chemical ethers that were known by 1750 was a colorless and volatile liquid produced by the action of sulphuric acid upon alcohol. It was this substance that Dr. John C. Warren used at Massachusetts General Hospital on October 13, 1846, when removing a huge tumor from the neck of Gilbert Abbot.

Dr. William T. G. Morton, the dentist who had told Warren about the effects of the chemical, served as anesthesiologist for that historic operation. He used a homemade inhalator to administer the ether.

With his partner, Charles Jackson, a Boston chemist, Morton obtained a fourteen-year patent using the trade name Letheon. Jackson sold his interests to Morton for 10 percent of all profits realized. Congress considered offering Morton $100,000 for "his" chemical, but many scientists protested that he had no proprietary rights. Morton (now known to have been four years behind Georgia's Dr. Crawford W. Long in the use of ether as an anesthetic) clung to his patent and became embittered during years of futile attempts to collect royalties.

TUBERCLE BACILLUS

German bacteriologist Robert Koch won fame as a result of his work on anthrax, a disease that affects cattle. In the course of that investigation he developed ways to dye various kinds of microbes. This was fundamental to identification of germs under the microscope, and so proved of tremendous value to research workers.

Even the great Robert Koch had no success when he tried to make visible the microorganism that he was sure caused tuberculosis. Colleagues with international reputations practically laughed in his face; they were sure that tuberculosis was an illness caused by factors other than germs.

Just before he reached his fortieth birthday, Koch placed a single slide in a solution of blue methylated spirits—then forgot about it. Since the bottle of dye had been uncorked for a long time, he didn't expect it to be usable.

The next day the bacteriologist gave a perfunctory glance through his microscope, then stared in astonishment at seeing clusters of fine, blue-dyed fibrils. He tried again with fresh dye but got no results. But with ammonia added the compound acted like the old solution made strong by evaporation.

Koch's chance find not only revealed the organism that came to be called the *tubercle bacillus*; it made possible a still continuing scientific attack on the cause of tuberculosis.

ANIMAL ELECTRICITY

The nerves of a frog played a crucial role in a drama that took place just before the turn of the nineteenth century. Italian physician Luigi Galvani, who was interested in the expanding field of physics, kept up with developments in that science. He knew that electricity was destined to become a major force in communication and in the distribution of power, but he agreed with his colleagues who took it for granted that electricity is generated and transmitted only in nonliving systems.

Galvani was interrupted during his dissection of a frog one day. The legs of the animal, temporarily fastened to a copper wire, were caught in a breeze that made them swing against an iron balcony railing. At the instant of contact the legs—dead by every known standard—twitched exactly as though they were alive.

Galvani pondered the strange reaction and correctly decided that it was electrical in nature. He didn't know enough physics to realize that the current was created by the differential between two kinds of metal (copper and iron), but underscored the importance of the fact that electrical forces operate within living bodies.

His triumphant demonstration that "animal electricity" is a real rather than an imaginary force paved the way to modern absorption with intricate and low-level electrical reactions that play so large a part in the functioning of the human body.

STETHOSCOPE

Regarded as an essential instrument in the modern practice of medicine, the stethoscope owes its existence to a bizarre combination of chance plus the modesty of a young French physician.

René Laënnec was consulted one day by a rather buxom young woman who complained of pains in her chest. Her description indicated the possibility of heart trouble.

Physicians of the era, like their predecessors who had for centuries tried to diagnose heart conditions by listening to beating of the organ, had just two ways to get information. One was percussion—tapping on the patient's chest and listening to the sounds made. The other was by application of the ear to the patient's chest.

"The patient's age and sex did not permit me to resort to direct application of the ear to the chest," Laënnec later said in a written summary of his experience.

Shortly after this incident he was relaxing in a Paris park. Children playing near him "tapped" signals to one another from opposite ends of a hollow log. In a flash of insight, Laënnec realized that a tubular wooden apparatus would permit him to hear heartbeat and chest sounds at a properly modest distance.

Before the end of 1816 he had perfected the world's first stethoscope, a wooden tube with an earpiece that actually transmitted sounds from heart and chest more clearly than the means formerly used, applying the physician's ear to the patient's skin.

CIRCULATION OF THE BLOOD

Long regarded as the seat of life and consequently important in religion as well as in medicine, blood was known to move long before anyone knew how or why it flows. One of the first attempts to analyze the vital current came from the pen of Spanish physician Michael Servetus, who was burned at the stake as a religious heretic by Calvinists of Switzerland.

Servetus attempted to describe the way blood circulates through the lungs, but he ignored other parts of the body. A few investigators who worked in the early part of the seventieth century had vague notions that linked the pumping action of the heart with movements of blood, but anything approaching real understanding was lacking.

William Harvey, physician to the court of England, became intrigued with the riddle of the blood's movement and made the first comprehensive scientific study of it. From the dissection of animals, Harvey concluded that blood is pumped through veins and arteries by the heart.

This notion—which challenged long accepted ideas, according to which the heart manufactures blood—was too radical for most persons. Harvey withheld publication of his findings for twelve years, but finally issued a seventy-two page book in 1628 at the insistence of a friend. Many medical experts, notably members of the faculty of a famous medical school in Paris, scoffed at the notion that the blood is in continuous circulation. General acceptance of the concept didn't come until about 1700—more than eighty years after Harvey had charted the course followed by the stream of life.

BLOOD TRANSFUSION

Medieval physicians attached great importance to the quantity of blood in the bodies of patients. They considered many maladies to stem from an excess of the fluid, and so made bloodletting or "leeching" standard treatment in many conditions.

There were circumstances, however, a few pioneers agreed, in which a person had too little blood rather than too much. Would it be possible, somehow, to transfer the life-bearing fluid from one body to another?

England's Richard Lower thought it could be done, so made some attempts to transfuse blood from one dog to another. In Paris, the noted Jean-Baptiste Denis decided to try a far more radical procedure. Attempting to save the life of a man weakened by bleeding, late in 1666, the physician succeeded in transfusing blood from a lamb into the veins of the patient. After seeming to improve, the patient died in agony.

Horrified members of the Paris medical faculty banned any additional attempts at blood transfusion; soon their decision was strengthened by a papal edict.

Reaction against transfusion of the blood of an animal into a human (inevitably dangerous and now known to be an invitation to a fatal reaction) was so great that the idea languished for generations. Even when transfusion was revived and successfully carried out between human donors and recipients, the knowledge of blood types was in its infancy so adverse reactions were common and serious.

THE BRAIN AS SEAT OF INTELLIGENCE

Many scholars consider the oldest of surgical textbooks to be the papyrus document, now lost, whose instructions are transmitted by the Edwin Smith papyrus. Findings incorpo-rated in these pioneer books date from 3000 B.C. or earlier Many of the observations they contain are still valid.

One of the most important is a section on the brain, whose convolutions are described in some detail. Clearly and without ambiguity, the ancient writer or writers indicate that "the brain is the seat of intelligence and mental functions."

How many colleagues shared this view that was advanced by some Egyptian pioneer or the members of the ancient equivalent of a clinic, no one knows. The document did circulate rather widely, but the link between brain and thought was later forgotten or repudiated. For many centuries medical experts would have risked their reputations on the view that a person's thoughts are associated with his heart.

The "discovery" of the true function of the brain, therefore, represented rediscovery of knowledge that had been lost or ignored for centuries.

OPENING OF THE SKULL

Archaeological finds from widely scattered areas give positive evidence that ancient medicine men opened the skulls of many who consulted them. Many operations of this sort were performed in Stone Age cultures where metal surgical instruments were not available. What's more, at least some patients survived to have a second round of the same surgery.

Known to doctors as trephining, the practice of cutting a hole in the skull yielded an approximately circular piece of bone, or rondelle. Rondelles from trephined skulls were widely used as amulets and were sometimes strung together to form necklaces.

All this took place long before the beginning of recorded history.

Lacking written records and explanations, there is no positive understanding of the motives that prompted a worldwide surge of operations upon skulls. An educated guess rests on the fact that virtually all ancient and primitive peoples linked illness with "possession by demons." That being the case, a person troubled with a splitting headache that wouldn't quit would appear to be the victim of an evil spirit. Cutting a hole in such a person's skull (and going through the proper rites of exorcism) at least created a chance that the demon would leave and never come back.

No other interpretation gives an acceptable explanation for the astonishing extent to which Stone Age medicine men mastered the art of opening skulls.

SYPHILIS

Syphilis is the only major disease named through the impact of a fable written to account for its origin.

Since "the accursed dishonourable disease" appeared in Europe just before the beginning of the sixteenth century, some medical historians think it was brought back from the New World by members of Columbus' crew. Whether that was the case or not, Italy was hit earlier and harder than any other nation.

Physicians compared the dreadful new malady with smallpox, but recognized that it was a distinct disease. Noblemen and members of royalty were stricken as well as common soldiers and tavern rowdies. Some authorities list several dozen kings plus two popes (Alexander VI and Julius II) whose medical histories indicate that they were infected.

Using a type of propaganda often linked with major ills, Germans and Italians called the malady "the French Evil." Girolamo Fracastoro of Verona wrote a mythological poem to account for the origin of the new disease. In the 1530 version of his epic, the hero was a Greek shepherd, Syphilus. Tormented by the sun one day, he cursed the sun god Helios and raised an altar to his own king. Helios punished Syphilus by striking him with an unknown disease.

Named for a wholly fictional character in a tale not intended to be taken seriously, the disease that may have been endemic in the New World before the arrival of the white man annually claims hundreds of thousands of new victims.

TULAREMIA

In his 1845 journey to Los Angeles, California pioneer John Sutter traveled for a whole month across a vast *tulare,* or plain of tules (bulrushes). Eventually the name of the plant attached to a county.

Tulare County attracted little attention until early in the present century. Then its name entered the lexicon of medicine.

As a precautionary measure after the San Francisco fire of 1906, the U.S. Public Health Service examined many rats and squirrels for evidence of bubonic plague. They found none. But ground squirrels from a wide region proved to be infected with an unknown bacillus whose effects were suggestive of those caused by plague.

All attempts to identify the disease were futile, so for a time it was known simply as "the plague-like disease of rodents." In 1912, laboratory workers isolated the bacterium involved and found it to be a minute rod-shaped organism. Since their work was concentrated in Tulare County at the time of this discovery, the disease took the name of the region.

Now known to be extremely dangerous to humans and not merely a menace to rodents in obscure Tulare County and surrounding regions, tularemia (or "rabbit fever") ranks high on the list of ills that threaten hunters and outdoorsmen.

PLACEBO

At least as early as the thirteenth century, English priests made frequent use of a special rite or "office" performed for the benefit of the dead. Sung or chanted rather than spoken, the majestic words echoed through many an abbey as evensong was finished and twilight fell.

In the Latin version of Psalm 114:9 the opening line in the first antiphon (or devotional verse sung responsively by two choirs) read: *Placebo Domino in regione vivorum* ("I will walk before the Lord in the land of the living").

From the opening word the rite itself was popularly known

155

as "the placebo." Since it was celebrated for the sake of the dead (usually in order to please the living), the placebo came to be linked with concepts of servility and flattery.

Any sycophant was likely to be described as "singing the placebo." In his *Merchant's Tale*, 1386, Chaucer used the term much as modern persons use "parasite." Numerous religious tracts—of Protestant origin—later attacked followers of the pope as "placebos and flatterers."

Long before the rise of psychosomatic medicine, physicians often found themselves in a dilemma. A patient for whom one had no specific remedy, and whose illness was vague or undefined, was likely to demand medicine. Sugar pills were the most common palliatives prescribed in such a situation, but various innocuous herbs were also used.

By the nineteenth century any inert medicament was being called a placebo; far from dwindling in importance, placebos still are prescribed in enormous numbers.

CAESAREAN SECTION

Myths that predate written history by many centuries are full of tales involving the cutting of babies from bodies of their mothers. Asclepius, god of sleep in Greek tales, was cut by his father Apollo from the body of the dying Coronis. Numerous other figures, half human and half divine, are said to have been delivered in this fashion.

Traditions that ascribe the birth of Julius Caesar to a successful surgical operation gave the name to the modern procedure.

In historical times, the operation actually was practiced down through the ages, but until the year 1500 only upon dying mothers. England's King Edward VI, only son of Henry VIII, was cut from the body of the dying Jane Seymour as late as 1537.

The first recorded caesarean delivery involving a mother who survived the ordeal was accomplished not by a physician, but by a Swiss butcher of pigs and hogs. Jacob Nufer knew how to use a knife. His wife, being unable to deliver her child, was rapidly approaching a crisis. Barber-surgeons refused to operate so long as the woman was living; midwives took the same stand.

The desperate husband opened up his wife, delivered the baby, and stitched the wounds of the mother as best he could. Her child lived—and so did she, to become the mother of four other babies. It wasn't until the development of modern anesthetics and aseptic methods of surgery that the caesarean section became safe and common.

CATGUT

Wounds suffered by ancient hunters and warriors are believed to have inspired the idea of deliberately cutting into the bodies of the sick. Prehistoric surgeons soon learned that big incisions wouldn't heal properly unless the parts were somehow held together.

A variety of techniques were tried. One of the most unusual was the use of huge ants. Insects were permitted to bite along an incision; then their heads were clipped off to form crude but surprisingly effective surgical clamps.

Experiments with materials used in weaving and in sewing demonstrated that the human body is powerless to absorb most common substances of this sort. Hemp, thin strips of leather, and even string made of wool cause sores that may be worse than the wound or incision that has been sewn together.

At least eighteen hundred years ago, and probably much earlier, surgeons experimented with thin strips made from the intestines of sheep. Instead of causing flesh to "fester" at each puncture, this material was absorbed by the body in about ninety days. We now know that this reaction is due to the action of certain enzymes in the human body.

Ancient surgeons didn't know anything about enzymes, but when they found a method that worked they were smart enough to follow it. Untold numbers of patients have been stitched up with strips from the intestines of sheep, cattle, and even horses.

For no logical reason—except that the dried strips seem too small to come from big animals—the surgeon's material came

157

to be universally known as catgut. There is no record that the intestines of cats have ever been successfully used in surgery!

PRESCRIPTIONS

Long before physicians began jotting down terse formulas intelligible only to pharmacists, the custom of listing the ingredients to be used in medicines was firmly established.

Much evidence suggests that the earliest of prescriptions were the personal property of the physicians who used them to compound their own remedies. Usually secret and often valuable, such prescriptions were never seen by patients.

One of the oldest prescriptions in the United States is preserved in New York's Metropolitan Museum of Art, and dates from about 1500 b.c. Precise directions for grinding and mixing precious stones are given on both sides of a smooth piece of limestone or ostracon.

Until comparatively modern times the majority of physicians dispensed their own medicines. Any man who had an enviable record of remarkable cures was likely to be credited with having devised or bought some rare prescription whose nature was jealously guarded as a professional secret.

The development of apothecary shops devoted chiefly or exclusively to the preparation and sale of drugs paved the way for the prescription scribbled on a sheet of paper.

SCIENTIFIC ANATOMY

A Greek physician of the second century settled in Rome about a.d. 164. His strategic location at the crossroads of the world plus his genuine gifts as a writer contributed to the fact that Galen produced at least two hundred medical works, or "books." Portions of more than a hundred of them have been preserved through the centuries.

The prestige of Galen was so great that his books were taken as the final source of authority by Greek, Roman, and even

Arabic physicians. One of his most famous works was an elaborate treatise on human anatomy.

Viewed by modern eyes, this famous work had just one major flaw. Most of Galen's detailed descriptions were based on the dissections of monkeys rather than men. As a result, for more than a thousand years Western medicine was hampered by gross errors about the makeup of the body.

Belgian anatomist Andreas Vesalius, one of the first moderns actually to dissect the human body, became so outraged by the errors of Galen that he spent years writing the first scientific volume about human anatomy. Called *Fabrica*, it was issued in 1543 by Johannes Oporinus, the most noted Swiss printer of the era.

Today this pioneer volume that put the study of anatomy on a scientific basis is regarded as among the greatest if not the very greatest medical book ever published. But when issued more than four hundred years ago, it created a storm of protest. Conservatives everywhere objected to making any changes in anatomy as described by the great Galen.

RUBBER GLOVES

Today no patient in the Western world would voluntarily undergo surgery without being sure that the wielder of the knife would wear sterile rubber gloves.

These now universal accessories were developed as a result of the fact that a nurse at Johns Hopkins Hospital had a nineteenth-century forerunner of "detergent hands." Every time she scrubbed up for an operation the strong antiseptic she was required to use caused her skin to break out in a rash.

Dr. William Halstead, chief of the hospital's surgical staff, decided that desperate measures were in order. He made plaster casts of the nurse's hands, then took the casts to a major rubber company and had thin gloves molded from them. They put an end to her irritated hands and fostered a budding romance between the nurse and Dr. Halstead that eventually led to marriage.

Dr. Halstead liked the gloves used by his wife so much

that about 1893 he made casts of his own hands and ordered gloves. He was probably the first person in the world to wear them while cutting upon the body of a patient.

More sterile than even the best-scrubbed hands, gloves were adopted by Halstead's colleagues and students, creating so large a market that individually molded pairs of them gave way to standard sizes that now cost a few cents a pair.

ALLERGY

No one knows how many millions of persons suffer from acute forms of allergy. Some specialists doubt that anyone is 100 percent immune from low-level allergic reactions.

Yet this phenomenon that is now a focal point of continuous research was not clearly described until this century.

French physiologist Charles Richet was seeking to determine the toxic dose of poison from a sea anemone. Using an extract of the animal's tentacles, in 1898 he made laboratory tests on a number of dogs. Some of Richet's animals died. After the survivors recovered he gave them much smaller doses of the same chemical. To his astonishment all of them became ill; one big animal named Neptune died from a dose that the scientist considered to be far below the lethal level.

Richet pondered the riddle of Neptune's death, and concluded that it was due to "induced sensitization." That is, the second exposure to extract from the sea anemone produced a reaction whose violence was due to bodily changes brought about by the first exposure.

Richet's experiments involved intravenous injections. He and his scientific colleagues soon realized that a related condition, allergy, can be rooted in exposure to practically anything in the environment—from egg yolk to house dust and the hair of pets. "Induced sensitization" soon loomed so large in medicine that Richet was awarded the Nobel prize for 1913; today allergy ranks among the half-dozen most common causes for a visit to the doctor.

PENICILLIN

Quite by accident, one of the miracles of modern medicine occurred in a London laboratory in 1928.

Bacteriologist Alexander Fleming was working with a culture of deadly staphylococcal germs, which are responsible for blood poisoning, boils, carbuncles, and many other maladies.

Fleming's petri dish containing the potent broth was sitting close to an open window. The wind blew minute particles through that window and some of them settled on the laboratory vessel. A few hours later, Fleming noticed, with astonishment, that many of the staphylococcal germs were dead. On the spot he concluded that some unknown microorganism had fallen into the petri dish—and had thrived in the germs it contained.

It took a decade of intensive work to extract a wee amount of the active principle from the mold that chanced to be blown by the wind into Fleming's laboratory. Purified, the compound became known as penicillin—first of the great antibiotics.

Now prescribed with caution because of its own potential side-effects, penicillin, whose discovery was triggered by chance, has revolutionized the production and use of germ-controlling agents. Incredibly, the most potent U.S. strain of penicillin was developed from microorganisms found on a rotten cantaloupe in the fruit market of Peoria, Illinois.

RELIEF FOR MOTION SICKNESS

For reasons still not fully understood, great numbers of persons become ill as a result of being subjected to continuous motion. During the days of the great sailing vessels, it often took a new hand several weeks to "get his sea legs," or conquer motion sickness. As late as World War II, the transportation of large numbers of men by sea made motion sickness a paramount—and unsolved—problem of military medicine.

In 1947 allergist Leslie N. Gay treated a patient with a new antihistamine marketed under the trade name Dramamine. The patient had taken only a few doses before she reported a puzzling reaction. For some odd reason she no longer became dizzy on her ride to the doctor's office.

Gay checked her story and decided it was accurate, so he tested the compound, known to chemists as dimenhydrinate, upon a few volunteers. They too reported that it prevented motion sickness.

Discovered because a patient was alert enough to notice unusual effects, the wholly unexpected impact of Dramamine far overshadowed its role as an antihistamine. By the 1950's the chemical was in wide use by travelers on land, on water, and in the air.

Measure for Measure

FINGER

In English-speaking nations the finger or digit, now used chiefly as a measurement for alcoholic beverages, was the basic unit of many ancient systems.

Tomb sculptures from pre-Christian dynasties in Egypt clearly indicate that the width of a man's index finger was one of the earliest standards to enter general use. Early Egyptian digits had a mean length of .728 inches; in Assyria, the same unit measured .730 inches; and it averaged .734 inches in Persia.

CUBIT

No longer in use and remembered chiefly because it figures largely in Scripture, the cubit was the basic unit of measurement of the ancient construction worker. He carried his standard of measurement about with him; in order to determine a cubit he had only to put his arm flat against a surface and mark the distance from the tip of his middle finger to his elbow.

Many biblical measurements, notably those employed by Noah in building the ark, are given in cubits.

At the time the Great Pyramid was built, the Egyptian cubit varied from about 20.51 inches to 20.71 inches and had a mean length of 20.62 inches. It is the latter length that is accurately and precisely used in man's oldest monument.

For the sake of accuracy the length of the cubit was scratched

163

on many tombs and occasionally indicated on papyrus. For convenience, Egyptians often divided this vital unit into seven palms of twenty-eight digits—though twenty-eight of their digits didn't measure precisely a cubit.

Archaeologists haven't yet found cubit measures in Palestine. Considerable evidence indicates that the Israelites used the unit created by Egyptians, who marked the nineteenth digit, about fourteen inches. There were substantial variations, though, which rule out absolute precision in translating the size of Og's bed (Deuteronomy 3:11) and the height of Goliath (1 Samuel 17:4). The reconstruction of Solomon's Temple can be made to scale, but lack of certainty about the cubit used by his architects makes it impossible to know the exact size of the building.

FOOT

Measurements based upon or determined by parts of the human body were used long before they were given formal names. Such a handy unit, intermediate between a very small and a quite long one, was provided by the human foot.

Tradition says that the size of the foot, the most widely used of all modern units of length, was determined by using the foot of Charlemagne as a standard. Since the conqueror was tall, the English foot is substantially longer than comparable units used in some civilizations.

Regardless of whose foot or feet were used in arriving at a standard, most peoples have succeeded in keeping variations at a relatively low level. During a period of three hundred years, the Roman foot in Italy varied an average of 1/400 from the mean. The English foot was even more uniform and was stabilized within narrow limits long before the rise of sophisticated modern measuring devices.

As late as the eighteenth century more than two hundred variants of the foot existed in Europe. These created no problems until manufactured goods entered markets of more than local impact. International trade was seriously handicapped by variations that weren't reduced to workable levels until modern times. Even today in parts of Canada, the French foot, which is equivalent to 12.8 English inches, remains in local use.

HAND

Owners and managers of fine horses still measure the height of animals in hands, but for all other purposes this relic from antiquity is obsolete.

As used in the Near East the handbreadth, or palm, indicated the breadth of one's hand at the base of the fingers. Since men's hands are typically wider than those of women, only males employed this unit.

Arbitrarily fixed by present-day horse lovers at four inches, the hand occasionally mentioned in Scripture (Ezekiel 40:43; Exodus 25:25) is believed to have measured about 2.9 inches.

SPAN

Long before standards of weight and measurement became matters of international concern, artisans found that they needed a unit longer than a hand but not so long as a cubit. Naturally they turned to their own bodies to find it.

The distance from the tip of a man's thumb to the tip of his little finger, when his fingers are outspread, became known as the span. Treated in practice as equivalent to one-half cubit, the span minutely described by the prophet Ezekiel measured about 10.2 inches. In the English-speaking world it is now treated as 9.0 inches in length.

Ancient narrators who described the epic bout between David and Goliath didn't want their readers to think they were estimating the height of the Philistine champion, so they specified his height as exceeding six cubits by a span.

Long abandoned as a unit of measurement, span is still used as both a noun and a verb in common speech.

YARD

Youthful by comparison with such units as the finger and the foot, the yard probably developed as a by-product of the weaver's trade. In order to measure tapestry or cloth, a craftsman found it easy to extend one arm while simultaneously grasping his product with his teeth and moving unmeasured segments forward with his other arm.

This practice probably accounts for the fact that the yard was commonly treated as the distance between a man's nose and the tips of his fingers. Tradition holds that the English standard was determined by King Henry I, who obligingly used his own body to establish it.

Widely used to measure the shots of archers as well as other distances, the yard varied even more than most other units until it was standardized at three feet, or thirty-six inches.

In Great Britain the standard yard is the distance between two transverse lines on gold plugs in a bronze bar, at 62°F., kept at the Standards Office of the Board of Trade. Americans, for no logical reason, base their standard yard upon the meter. In this country, therefore, the yardstick by which all other yards are measured is 0.9144018 meter.

FATHOM

Just as the yard measure spontaneously emerged from the ways workmen handled leather and textiles, so the fathom was the natural product of casting out and hauling in long lines.

Seamen needed some unit of measurement that was adapted to their work and could be applied quickly. The length of the outstretched arms, from tip of one middle finger to tip of the other middle finger, was just right for the measurement of lines.

Now standardized to six feet, the fathom has such strong links with the sea that it is often used to indicate depths. Miners once measured the depth of coal seams and deposits of metal in fathoms, and the seaborn unit was also applied to stacks of wood. These usages are now all but obsolete, and the fathom is even losing its place in the lingo of seamen, who are prone to use feet or meters in lieu of the ancient unit.

NAUTICAL MILE

Since legionnaires of ancient Rome had no way of marking off one thousand paces on the surface of a lake or ocean, the nautical mile was at best a haphazard thing. All attempts to measure long distances across the water by "triangulation" failed, so the best that an early ship's master could do was to offer a guesstimate.

The development of the metric system complicated the situation about the time mariners had agreed that a nautical mile should be defined as equal to the length of one minute of arc along the circumference of our planet.

The length of the earth's circumference varies according to whether equatorial or polar measurements are used. So it helped very little to stipulate that a nautical mile should be treated as equal to 1/21,600th of the planet's circumference.

Founders of the metric system had employed a particular quadrant, made famous by their work. As a compromise, therefore, the International Hydrographic Bureau proposed that the nautical mile be measured along the same line that is the base of the metric system. Adoption of this system yielded a nautical mile equal to 6,076.097 feet.

Until the dawn of the Space Age, landsmen had little interest in or concern with the mile as measured by mariners. It is the nautical rather than the statute (or land) mile, however, that is employed in most calculations of distances in space. Elevated to a new role by voyagers to the moon, the "long mile" may eventually make the statute mile obsolete.

INCH

Reasonably exact measurement of distances less than the width of a finger pose problems not readily soluble by relying upon the human body. Peoples of many cultures have used the seeds of cultivated grains as units. Few such units have had lasting influence since they varied according to the type of grain grown in a particular locality.

Barley proved to be an exception to this general rule. Grains of barley are remarkably uniform and conveniently small. They were used in many kinds of precise measurement, and their influence has persisted into the Space Age. Shoe sizes are still generally measured in terms of barleycorns; a size ten shoe is one barleycorn longer than a size nine.

Since twelve is fundamental to the Roman system of counting, it was natural for regions under Roman influence to divide the foot into twelve segments. This unit, the inch, was specified as constituting "the length of three standard barleycorns laid end to end." Only after the exact length of the foot was stabilized and became generally adopted did the inch sometimes fall short of or exceed the length of three grains of barley.

FURLONG, MILE

Agriculture's central role in medieval life is attested to by a seldom-used unit of measurement that grew out of the habits of plowmen and that helped shape one of the most common distances used in the English-speaking world.

Farmers of Britain commonly built stone walls to separate fields whose length had been standardized before written records were kept. Allowing space to turn his animals at each end of a row, the plowman typically plowed furrows equal to about 220 modern yards. Slurring of the term "furrow-long" in common speech resulted in furlong being used as a label for the length of a furrow.

Today the use of furlong is practically defunct, except on the racetrack, where it may determine the distance horses must run. It had far-reaching impact, however, in determining the length of a mile when natives of Britain decided to adopt the mile as their longest unit in common use.

Romans had measured miles in terms of one thousand paces by a marching soldier. This distance approximated five-thousand feet. But such a distance can't be divided into an even number of furlongs; it yields about seven and a half. Unwilling to budge from the length of their long cherished furlong, the people of Britain insisted that a mile should be made up of eight of them. This produced a unit of 1,760 yards or 5,280 feet.

METER

In the aftermath of the French Revolution, scientific leaders of that country scrapped existing systems of measurement (which were about as chaotic and complex as those used in the English-speaking world) and decided to put everything on a decimal system.

Their new standard of length, the metre, was easily modified to English meter. Seeking what they considered the most stable base on which to erect the system, scholars settled on the circumference of the earth.

Distance from the equator to the north pole was calculated —along a line running through Paris. One ten-millionth of this distance was arbitrarily designated as the metre. It was assumed that if the standard metre made to serve as a guide for measuring instruments should ever be destroyed, it could always be duplicated from measurements of the earth.

Today we know that eighteenth-century calculations weren't quite accurate. The distance from the North Pole to the equator—by way of Paris—is actually 10,002,288 meters. To make matters worse, the size and shape of our planet are in slow but constant change.

169

That's why the eleventh General Conference on Weights and Measures, in 1960 (in Paris!), redefined the meter. Now it indicates 1,650,763.73 wavelengths in a vacuum of a particular emission line of the chemical isotope, krypton 86. For practical purposes, the new unit, which is identical with the old "standard meter," permits greater accuracy in making new meter-sticks.

LIGHT-YEAR

Early attempts to measure distances in "outer space"—beyond our solar system—were unsatisfactory. Things changed in 1838.

That year Friedrich Bessel of Königsberg Observatory succeeded in measuring the distance from the earth to a star that astronomers label *61 Cygni*. Bessel made observations in January and in July (at opposite extremities of the base of Earth's orbit) and then measured the apparent shift in position of the star.

Earth's orbit had already been measured with reasonable accuracy. Data about it plus the apparent (not actual) shift in position of *61 Cygni* enabled the astronomer to calculate that the star is 60 million million miles from Earth.

As more and more long-distance measurements accumulated, the clumsiness of applying the mile to cosmic distances became apparent.

In March, 1888, scientists adopted a new standard—the only

one in general use that exceeds the mile and the kilometer. To measure distances in space, astronomers agreed, the only workable unit is the light-year, or the distance light travels in a vacuum in one year. Usually treated as 5,878,000,000,000 miles, or 5.878 trillion miles, or 5.878×10^{12} miles, the light-year is measured to four or five decimal places when real precision is required.

GRAIN

The accurate measurement of gold, silver, precious stones, and other valuables required a small but precise unit of weight. Englishmen found something growing in their fields that could be used as such a unit. Few small objects are so uniform in weight as grains of wheat taken from the middle of "well-formed ears."

For centuries the grain ruled supreme; it was this unit that determined the weight of a pound, rather than vice versa. Established in 1270, and made legal for all commodities except gold, silver, and medicines, the merchant's pound consisted of precisely 6,750 grains.

Whether the average size of wheat grew smaller or the pound became larger is uncertain, but by Elizabethan times the latter unit was measured by 7,002 grains. Today's pound avoirdupois has been standardized at 7,000 grains. Both the pound troy and the apothecaries' pound are substantially lighter with just 5,760 grains.

Long used in coinage as well as by dealers in precious commodities, the grain is now seldom encountered except in dealings with pharmacists and jewelers. Aspirin, for example, has nothing whatever to do with wheat, but the size of the tablets has been standardized at five grains for adults.

CARAT

As a shortcut in handling costly merchandise, Arabic tradesmen adopted a unit believed to have been based on the weight

171

of a native bean. Four times as heavy as a grain, this seed—or carat—became especially important in measuring pearls, diamonds, and other jewels.

For no known reason, medieval goldsmiths adopted the unit earlier employed by jewelers but treated it as equal to twelve grains rather than four.

One of the most important gold coins of medieval Europe, the mark, was supposed to be of pure metal equal in weight to twenty-four carats (or 288 grains). Circulation of this coin established 24-carat as a standard for purity of gold.

Since the ancient standard clings tenaciously to life, a present-day manufacturer who produces 10-carat gold tie clips is offering a product that is 10/24 gold.

At the jewelry store, however, the earlier and smaller carat still reigns. Until it was standardized it didn't vary much—but it doesn't take much diamond to make a difference. Consequently, modern dealers in precious stones have resorted to the metric system and established the carat that they use as equal to 200 mg., a mass virtually identical with 3.086 standardized grains.

GALLON

Some type of early container that could be produced in quantity—probably but not certainly a pottery dish or basin—established the gallon as a unit of liquid measure.

Obviously the gallon lacked the stability of units such as the foot and the grain; potters could make vessels whose size varied a great deal more than those of human feet or grains of wheat.

Long after the gallon had become widely adopted, confusion about its size reigned supreme. Makers and sellers of wine used a relatively small gallon, while persons who sold meal and other cheap commodities used gallons of generous size.

This thoroughly bewildering state of affairs has left its imprint upon the modern world. In the United States, the old wine gallon of 231 cubic inches is the standard, but in Britain and former British colonies the "imperial" gallon of 277.274 cubic inches is commonly used.

If you rent a car in England and buy gasoline (petrol) by the gallon you'll find the price outrageously high. But it will be some small solace to remember that, after all, you're getting bigger gallons!

QUART, PINT

Long before there was a general effort to standardize the size of the gallon, a haphazard unit of volume that varied according to the size of vessels produced by potters, practical considerations demanded the development of smaller units.

One fourth of a gallon could hardly be called anything but *quart* in lands influenced by Latin.

Quart-size vessels, approximating one-fourth the capacity gallon containers, were probably produced as household utensils that later doubled as measuring vessels.

Even this quantity was too big for convenience in handling scarce and costly liquids. A quart vessel with a line painted or marked at the midpoint provided measurement in terms of the unit we know as the *pint*, named for the paint used to indicate it.

Since national standardization failed to bring international agreement about the size of the gallon, it was inevitable that the same confusion should attach to quarts and pints. The British or "imperial" pint is equivalent to .57 liters or 34.66 cubic inches; the U.S. standard pint is .47 liters or 28 7/8 cubic inches. U.S. beer drinkers accustomed to ordering by the pint are especially impressed by the difference the first time they down a pint secured in a British pub.

FIFTH

From the infancy of the republic, U.S. lawmakers have seized upon alcoholic beverages as good sources of revenue. Taxation began early, has never been reduced, but has often been increased.

Many eighteenth- and early nineteenth-century statutes stipulated the amount of federal, state, and local tax that had to be paid on a gallon or a quart of whisky. Makers and retailers saw a golden opportunity in the fact that for a period there was no tax on a quantity less than one quart.

It was this practical consideration that led to the development of a unit that is generally used only in the United States. By bottling their products in containers that held one-fifth of a gallon rather than the customary quart, many taxes were bypassed.

This state of affairs didn't last very long; lawmakers soon caught on and enacted new statutes establishing the amount of tax to be collected each time a fifth was sold. Before the loopholes were all closed, however, the queer unit that was born from a very special set of circumstances had become so well established in the liquor industry that the quart has never replaced the fifth.

OUNCE

If you have had even a smattering of Latin, you may have noticed that *ounce* bears a decided resemblance to the classical word for "twelve." Logic, therefore, would suggest that an ounce is 1/12 of an earlier and larger unit, perhaps the pound.

That would make complete sense except for the fact that we're accustomed to dealing with pounds made up of sixteen ounces rather than twelve.

How did such a tangled state of affairs come about?

Apothecaries were among the earliest merchants to be concerned with quantities much larger than a grain but substantially smaller than a pound. Influenced by Roman dependence upon the number twelve, they divided the pound that they used into twelve segments and called each an ounce.

This apothecaries' pound (or pound troy) was later supplanted by a substantially larger one. Medieval dealers in "goods of weight" such as meat, corn, and leather found the apothecaries' pound inconveniently small. In practice they found that a unit about one-third larger saved them a lot of time in weighing.

Since the ounce troy was already fairly well stabilized, it was natural to incorporate it into the new pound avoirdupois—whose size requried four additional ounces. That's why clerks in U.S. post offices, butcher shops, and many other establishments deal with a unit of one-sixteenth whose name means one-twelfth.

DEGREE

Many centuries ago Babylonian astronomers had accurate knowledge of the length of the year. Archaeological evidence indicates that some of them depicted the annual circuit of the sun about the sky by means of a circle divided into 365 equal parts.

Such a calendar (or predecessor of a calendar) was accurate enough for needs of the era. But the Babylonians were orderly people who knew a great deal about mathematics and liked to find mathematical precision in nature. In order to have a properly precise year made up of 360 days rather than the inconvenient 365, five days of each year were set aside as a holiday period and were not counted.

A circle divided into 360 equal parts lends itself nicely to all sorts of calculations; 360 can be divided evenly by 180, 120, 90, 72, 60, 45, 40, 36, 30, 24, 20, 18, 15, 12, 10, 9, 8, 6, 5, 4, 3, and 2.

Adoption of this stylized symbol for an artificially shortened year had such an impact upon civilization that circles of all kinds are still divided into precisely 360 degrees.

MINUTE, SECOND

Ancient measurements of the circular movement of the sun, achieved without any of the sophisticated instruments now employed, were astonishingly precise.

175

Once the 360-degree "circle of the sun" had been perfected, it was an easy step to divide again—and again. Here the number sixty was dominant. (Note that sixty is precisely one-sixth of 360, and that sixty is a multiple of twelve.)

Division of 1/360 of a circle into sixty parts, then dividing the product into sixty segments, produced a scale against which it was possible to plot the movement of the sun with great accuracy.

Overwhelming evidence indicates that astrologers worked with these segments of circles before the same pattern of division was applied to time. Minutes and seconds were in use for generations if not for centuries before the adoption of an hour made up of sixty minutes.

HOUR

Babylonians, who knew perfectly well that a year is made up of a bit more than 365 days, managed nicely with a calendar that counted only 360 of the days.

Archaeological research hasn't settled the question as to whether these ancient watchers of the sky knew the Earth revolves about the Sun, or thought the solar orb revolves about a central earth. Much evidence favors the former view.

Whatever their ideas about relative movements of Earth and Sun may have been, the Babylonians were so absorbed with observing and measuring apparent movement of the sun that 1/360 of a year was too clumsy a unit for practical use in casting horoscopes and reading the heavens.

Since the number twelve was basic to their system of counting, it was easy to divide the day into "two houses of twelve"—one of light and the other of darkness. Though light and dark dominate equal portions of the solar day only twice a year and Babylonians knew it, this system erected on the base of the number twelve became so thoroughly entrenched that it has persisted into the Space Age. Even those clocks and watches that are marked to indicate the full sweep from dawn to dawn continue to be divided into precisely twenty-four hours.

Customs

BLACK FOR MOURNING

Fast disappearing under the impact of liberalized religious views and the availability of multicolored clothing, the long-established custom of wearing black for mourning has nothing to do with Christian beliefs.

Actually, the color has never been universally used in Christendom and in many parts of the world is not linked with mourning. Yellow is the color of sorrow in Burma, while purple plays this role in many regions of China. Other Chinese insist that white should be worn during a period of mourning, but in Turkey the preferred color for transmitting the silent message "I have suffered the loss of a loved one" is violet.

The special role of black among Europeans and persons of European descent is believed due to pre-Christian superstitions. Early nature-worshipers (like the persons in most contemporary "primitive" societies) had a strong belief in immortality.

During the weeks immediately after a death there was danger that the soul of the deceased would return to former haunts and try to enter the body of someone found there. Probably in order to make it more difficult for ghosts to recognize them, relatives of a dead person wore black for a season.

Once established, the custom remained vital long after the factors that helped shaped it had been forgotten. Until comparatively recent times, therefore, the use of black for a period of mourning was observed "as a sign of respect for the dead," rather than a concession to dread that the recently departed spirit might return.

FISH ON FRIDAY

As a way of underscoring the centrality of Jesus' crucifixion, the church long ago established Friday as a weekly day of fasting. It was not enough to abstain from eating meat on the commemorative day; believers were expected to engage in acts of penance and even of physical mortification.

Astute students of ecclesiastical law pondered the regulations and raised the vexatious question: "Precisely what is meat?" Debated over and over in church councils, the question evoked a complicated set of rules. Their net effect was to classify all products of the sea as fish rather than meat.

Practical considerations may have affected the decisions of holy men, for in most Catholic countries great numbers of persons made their livelihood as fishermen.

One paradoxical effect of the ruling that food from the sea is not meat was a boost in consumption of steaks and other fine cuts from whales. Whales, as thoroughly mammalian as cattle, swine, and sheep, were by virtue of their mode of life classified by churchmen as "fish."

Turning to fish because meat was forbidden on the fast day, Christians gradually impressed the use of fish on Friday upon all Western civilization. Consequently (and paradoxically), contemporary Roman Catholic rulings that permit believers to eat real meat on Friday have had no observable effect upon the Friday consumption of fish.

RIGHT AND LEFT SHOES

Artisans had perfected the craft of shaping one sandal for the wearer's left foot and another for his right at least two thousand years before Christ. This much is clear from numerous archaeological finds.

Just when the practice fell into decay is uncertain. As populations grew, it became burdensome to shape shoes in this fashion. By the time of the Roman Empire, practically all commoners and the majority of soldiers were wearing shoes

179

made on straight lasts. Only patricians retained the custom of using gear made for each foot.

During the Middle Ages even kings and noblemen seldom had right and left shoes. The use of the straight last became standard among cobblers of all European nations.

Right and left shoes were revived for a comparatively brief period by dandies and great ladies of the Renaissance, but the straight last again dominated the shoe trade during American Colonial days.

Part of this wavering back and forth may have been a concession to changes in fashion; most of it was due to the inordinate amount of work required to turn out shaped shoes by hand. It wasn't until the 1850's and the introduction of machinery for making shoes that the use of right and left shoes became practically universal in the Western world.

Just when the final triumph of shaped shoes seemed assured, in the 1960's increasing numbers of rebels against inherited traditions stopped wearing shoes altogether.

CIGARETTE

European sailors and explorers probably experimented with various forms of tobacco soon after the plant was discovered in the New World. Some may have tried the South American practice of rolling finely cut tobacco to form a tube. Until the eighteenth century, however, no one left a record of such an experiment.

In his memoirs duelist-lover Giovanni Jacopo Casanova de Seingalt gave minute details about his exploits of all sorts. Buried in the eight-volume account is a report about an experiment in which he puffed smoke from Brazilian tobacco "wrapped in a little paper tube."

A few daring Italian and French smokers adopted the device tried by Casanova, but it wasn't until the 1850's that the cigarette began to challenge the familiar cigar.

Most historians attribute the spread of the cigarette to the Crimean War. Hundreds of thousands of English, Russian, and French troops gathered to oppose Turkish forces. Though the soldiers fought some of the bloodiest battles of modern times there were long periods in which they were idle. During these periods "little cigars" that men rolled for themselves at low cost gained such wide acceptance that they soon spread throughout Europe. From that base they jumped back to the New World, this time to North as well as South America.

COATS WITH SLIT TAILS

The sale of men's suits in the United States has been declining steadily for more than thirty years. A few clothiers are gloomily predicting the eventual disappearance of the suit made up of matched trousers and coat.

Coats themselves challenge this view and give silent witness to the power of tradition. Except for a few far-out models, most coats worn in the United States today are slit up the back. This practice stems directly from the era when gentlemen were accustomed to riding horses a great deal and couldn't get into saddles unless their coattails were slit.

Once firmly established in the garment trade, this usage retains its vitality in an era when ordinary folk ride horses only for pleasure and usually wear special clothing to do so.

PERPETUAL LIGHT

The use of a perpetual light at the grave of John F. Kennedy and at the final resting places of other notables represents a survival of practices that were started in the dim dawn of prehistoric times.

Thousands of years before men developed symbols with which to record their thoughts by means of writing, light was linked with the gods, with magic, and with life itself. In many regions it was essential to keep a fire burning at all times, for the fire meant protection from animals as well as cold. Methods of starting fires weren't sufficiently sophisticated to permit a family or tribe to stand by casually and let their fire die out.

By the time followers of Jehovah began shaping what was to

become the Hebrew-Christian tradition, light was so firmly linked with divinity that a lamp called *Ner Tamid* burned ceaselessly before the Ark of the Covenant (Leviticus 24:2-3). Symbolizing the physical presence of Jehovah and later the permanence of the Law of Moses, the perpetual flame came to be linked with the concept of hope even in times of death and distress. Perpetual lights have been used at the graves and tombs of many famous persons; at Arlington National Cemetery the flame that never goes out conveys to persons of the Space Age some of the indefinable ideas and moods by which Stone Age men groped toward God.

CHOIR

As a distinct dramatic form the tragedy was born about 535 B.C. That year, Greeks presented an elaborate public spectacle using three groups of trained dancers. From *choros* (dancing place) the entertainers who sometimes broke into song while dancing took a special name. The venerable term, having passed through Latin and Old French, entered English as "choir."

As early as the thirteenth century, many a cathedral had an elaborate choir. Singers were usually divided into two groups, one of which sat in the north and the other in the south side of the chancel. They sang in antiphonal fashion and were not accompanied by instruments. John Wycliffe, pioneer translator of the Bible, heard such a choir in 1380.

Members of the modern choir, far removed from the bands of Greek dancers who gave their name to such groups, seldom do anything more startling than whispering during the sermon.

FOUR-PANEL DOOR

During the Middle Ages most arts and crafts reached new heights of development. Workmen, organized into guilds, prided themselves on the perfection of handmade products.

It was a guild of English carpenters, according to widespread tradition, who made the first modern door. Their new device included four panels—two short upper ones and two long lower ones. Thick wood between the panels formed a clear and vivid cross.

No one knows whether the first panel door was designed in order to exhibit the Cross to every person who opened it, or whether the symbolism was the fruit of a new way of putting wood together. Whatever the case, the four-panel door remains a mute but eloquent bearer of Christendom's central symbol.

HIGH HEELS

Though they have enjoyed sporadic popularity in various epochs and among diverse peoples, high heels have been in continuous favor for a long period in only one culture—the modern West.

Strangely, it was a man rather than a woman who first used them. King Louis XIV of France was keenly conscious of the fact that he was shorter than most of his courtiers. To overcome this physical disadvantage he adopted high heels and wore them on many state occasions.

Influenced by the example of the gilded monarch, both men and women encouraged their bootmakers to experiment with new kinds of heels. Men gave up high heels when horseback riding went out of vogue, but great numbers of women still insist that most dress shoes be modeled after those of the French ruler.

CIGAR BANDS

Few common artifacts widely used in modern life are so colorful and intricate as cigar bands. Most persons throw them away; a few avid collectors scramble every time they glimpse what appears to be a new one.

These elaborate paper bands are now regarded as advertising pieces, though, originally, they performed an entirely different function.

Highborn ladies of Cuba and other Spanish territories smoked cigars freely during Colonial times. Experience taught them that tobacco was prone to stain their dainty white fingers.

Manufacturers of cigars struck back at this objection to nicotine by adopting the custom of placing narrow paper bands around their products. They effectively reduced the number of complaints about tobacco-stained fingers; soon, however, cigar makers saw they were losing an opportunity to call attention to their own brands. As a result, the design and manufacture of cigar bands have today developed into so complicated a system that, for practical purposes, it is a special form of heraldry.

ODD-PRICE SALES

Odd-price sales, which today are regarded as routine in the ceaseless struggle to lure customers, weren't born as a result of an attempt to make prices seem a trifle lower.

Melville E. Stone, the founder of the Associated Press, in 1876 decided that Chicago needed a penny newspaper to compete with those that sold for a nickel. A hasty survey indicated there would be plenty of buyers.

There was just one major stumbing block; relatively few pennies were then in circulation.

Stone, who was only twenty-eight years old, persuaded a number of leading merchants that an item priced at ninety-nine cents would sell faster than the same merchandise with a price tag of one dollar.

When some businessmen agreed to try the novel scheme, Stone made a personal trip to Philadelphia to get several barrels of pennies. The odd-price bargains that followed put pennies into circulation and made it easy for patrons to buy Stone's paper. Though his *Daily News* is still going strong, the impact of the merchandising technique Stone invented as a way of providing persons with coins to buy his papers has been far wider than that of the paper itself.

SCARECROW

Dionysus, Greek god of fertility, was considered to have such potency that even the crudest representation or image of him would cause fields to bear bigger crops.

Many farmers of classical times therefore erected at the edges of their fields little mannikins symbolizing Dionysus. Similar practices linked with gods and goddesses of fertility were observed in numerous other cultures whose people had no contact with the Greeks.

Long after nature-worship had lost its vitality, many rites associated with it were still practiced. One such holdover from antiquity was the age-old custom of putting a crude representation of a man (who couldn't be distinguished from the ancient gods) at the end of cultivated rows.

With the original function of the image forgotten, it came to be axiomatic that a manlike figure was helpful in frightening crows and other feathered thieves. Actually, there never has been a well-documented case study supporting the view that birds pay more attention to scarecrows than to other things.

Scientific questions about the practice notwithstanding, and with its origin in fertility rites long forgotten, farmers of many lands continue to use the scarecrow as a device to get better harvests by frightening away birds.

HANDSHAKE

Paradoxically, the handshake that Westerners have spread around the world as a symbol of mutual goodwill actually originated as a product of suspicion and distrust.

A medieval villager who chanced to meet a man he didn't know reacted automatically by reaching for his dagger. If the stranger did the same thing, the two were likely to spend a period cautiously circling around one another with blades in their hands.

When both became satisfied that the situation called for a parley instead of a fight to the finish, daggers were put back in their sheaths or laid on the ground. With his open hand extended to show that he did not hold a weapon, each man reached toward the other.

Evolving out of a desire to dispel fear, the handshake in Britain became what the kiss on each cheek is to the French and what the hearty rubbing of noses is to some South Sea Islanders.

CHRISTENING OF SHIPS

A ceremony in which a ship is christened was originally designed to do just what the name implies, that is, make the vessel Christian.

"Rites of blessing," as they were called by churchmen, were by ordinary folk regarded as baptismal ceremonies. Before being put to use, bells and other church furnishings went through ceremonial cleansing. As early as the tenth century the blessing of a bell was customarily reserved to a bishop, who washed the bell with holy water, signed it with oil of the sick on the outside, and then prayed that the inanimate messenger might bear good tidings.

The christening of ships, obviously closely linked with such rites of blessing, was especially important because pagans had been accustomed to bedecking a vessel with flowers on the day she was completed. Early ships often bore carved images of the gods and goddesses to whom they were dedicated in the

186

hope that divine influences would drive away bad luck. The figureheads which adorned many vessels until modern times are survivals of these ancient representations of divine figures.

Blessed by a holy man, sprinkled with consecrated oil, and given a Christian name, a ship was clearly under the protection of Jehovah. The wielding of champagne bottles by governmental leaders and other notables is a modern adaptation of the ancient rites that Christians earlier adapted from those of pagans.

BLUE RIBBON

Generations of searching for the specific factors that led to the establishment of England's most coveted decoration, the Order of the Garter, have yielded no final answers.

According to the official history (or Black Book) of the order itself, Richard the Lionhearted sought the aid of Saint George when his forces were employed against Cyprus and Acre. Through the instrumentality of the saint, the warrior king was inspired to tie leather thongs, or garters, about the legs of some of his knights. This inspired them to greater courage that led to victory. One of Richard's successors, King Edward III, fixed on this battlefield incident as inspiration for creating a new order of knights.

Another account that stems from the sixteenth century says that Edward III used his own garter as the signal to begin a battle in which he put the enemy to rout.

Still another conjecture, unsupported by earlier written evidence, but consistent with what is known about King Edward, suggests that in a crowded assembly a lady dropped her garter. Courtiers tittered, but the monarch placed the garter on his own knee and subsequently used it to name the order he founded.

Whatever the factors that produced the Order of the Garter, one thing is certain. From the beginning this highest of decorations was made with a band (or ribbon) of blue. Elevated into prominence in this fashion, the blue ribbon came to indicate the first rank in dog and horse shows, exhibits at county fairs, and practically every other form of contest popular in the English-speaking world.

CONFETTI

Today no all-out celebration or festival is complete without abundant use of confetti—colored paper cut into small pieces. However, a hero, dignitary, or honored guest showered with the original Italian confetti might have preferred to do without the honor, since confetti originally consisted of small hard bonbons. Merrymakers who participated in the carnival that preceded Lent (still observed in New Orleans and marked by special emphasis upon Mardi Gras) tossed these edible bits during parades and street festivals.

As the cost of making this kind of confetti rose and the demand for it increased, Italians substituted hard lime pellets about the size of hailstones. Carried around in a bag by maskers, confetti of this sort was thrown with a tin ladle.

By the time the citizens of Paris got around to tossing favors during pre-Lenten street festivals, it seemed much cheaper (and safer) to use paper confetti. Popularized by use during the "last fling" before the austerities of Lent were imposed, paper confetti—sometimes manufactured in colors for party use and sometimes improvised from ticker tape—has become a symbol of gaiety on any festive occasion.

BIRTHDAY CELEBRATIONS

Especially among persons of wealth and high rank, it was common in classical times to observe festivals in connection with anniversaries of birth.

Early Christians frowned on this practice, which was too closely linked with pagan customs to be given the approval of the church. Furthermore, the theology of the era stressed life as a necessary but transient time of testing. Death was welcomed as a deliverance. Consequently it is the deathday of a saint (the day on which he was born into heaven) that is celebrated in the calendar of the church.

Many early Christian references to "birthdays" must be read in the light of these views. "A birthday of a saint," wrote one early apologist, "has nothing to do with being born of earth, in the flesh. Instead it is that day on which a saint is born from earth into heaven, from labor to rest, from temptations to repose, from torments to delight."

So little interest focused on the day a person was born into this mortal life that there was no serious attempt to settle questions about the birthday of Jesus until the fourth century. It was another five hundred years before the birthday of the Holy Virgin was officially named.

Celebrations revolving about the birth of Christ became so popular and influential that the custom of celebrating birthdays of ordinary persons gradually spread throughout all Christendom.

CURFEW

Early European cities were often crowded with wooden houses with no chimneys; an open fire burned in the center of a dwelling or in its biggest room. It was for the sake of community safety that various rulers established laws requiring all citizens to cover their fires at a given signal.

Ancient city ordinances of London abound in stringent fire regulations. None was more effective, however, than the ringing of a "cover-fire" signal by church bells. This practice was followed at least as early as the time of King Alfred; traditions that credit its institution to William the Conqueror overlook the fact that he simply formalized much earlier customs.

Curfew signals were generally abandoned after "fireproof" building practices were instituted and fire-fighting equipment came into use.

Revived and given a new twist, the custom of establishing a curfew has helped cool off the hot climate of many a racial conflict. Though fires are no longer actually covered, the signal has the effect of ordering persons off the streets. Now transmitted by means of radio and television, and routinely applied to juveniles in many cities, the ancient signal that meant "put out the fire" can now be translated as ordering potential troublemakers to cool it.

TRICK OR TREAT

Once November 1 was designated as All Saints' or All Hallows' Day to honor those saints who do not have special days in the church calendar, it was inevitable that October 31 should come to play a new role. Since saints dominate November 1, logic suggests that witches, hobgoblins, and elves are busiest in the hours before they will have to take a back seat.

Halloween or All Hallow Even, known in some parts of England as Snapapple Night and Nutcrack Night, became a time for popular celebrations. Until modern times, all sorts of divination were practiced on this occasion—though the upcoming religious festival was never forgotten.

Especially in America, adults began turning their heads when youngsters seized the festive evening as a time for pranks. It became an unwritten law of the frontier that a boy or girl would go unpunished on Halloween for stunts that would not be tolerated during the rest of the year.

As a way of tempering the exuberance of youngsters, housewives began offering Halloween prowlers such delicacies as cookies, apples, and homemade candy in exchange for a promise that there would be no rough stuff. Born in America and still more widely observed here than anywhere else in the world, the call "trick or treat!" is youthful shorthand for a Halloween demand: "Unless you win me over by giving me a treat, you'll find your windows soaped or toilet paper draped across a tree on the morning of All Saints' Day."

APRIL FOOL

At first sight it makes no sense that a person's friends should try to make a fool of him on April 1 rather than on any other of the 365 days of the year. Light begins to glimmer, though, when you remember that March 25 was traditionally celebrated as New Year's Day. That meant that the first day of April was the octave, or semimagical eighth day of the feast. All ordinary work was suspended on that day; persons paid visits to old friends and new—with guest and host exchanging gifts at each encounter.

France led Christendom in shifting the beginning of the year to January 1. Adoption of the "reformed calendar" in 1564 meant that, for the French at least, the festivities that had been linked with the season of the New Year from time immemorial no longer took place in April.

Even though the once-central day in spring had lost its place of prominence, people still made a pretense of keeping up the old customs. That pretense took the form of playing tricks or conferring worthless gifts on friends. Since no one was immune

191

from such horseplay, the day was literally one on which all were fooled.

Spreading from France as its center, the custom of playing tricks—which appeals to the prankster innate in most persons —won general adoption. Now, long after the New Year festivities that once culminated on April 1 have been forgotten, the pseudo festivities that took their place continue to produce many an April fool.

BURNING IN EFFIGY

A practice that has been quiescent but is now enjoying a worldwide revival by persons belonging to militant groups of many kinds, burning in effigy is older than written history.

Some of the earliest accounts suggest that the custom was linked with concepts that are now associated with voodoo; that is, that the destruction of an image (however crude) that represented a specific person could injure or kill him.

Both wooden and wax figures have been used in many parts of the world by persons seeking to injure their enemies.

Burning (or hanging) a full-size figure made of straw or wood is a relatively modern practice. Guy Fawkes, a notorious figure in England's famous Gunpowder Plot, was probably the first person to be burned in effigy year after year. The custom of burning Judas in effigy was once widespread in Portuguese-dominated lands.

As part of traditional Fourth of July festivals, Benedict Arnold was burned in effigy almost everywhere that patriotic rallies were held. Many presidents, politicians, and military leaders got the same treatment. About the time that this offshoot of sorcery seemed to have died a natural death, persons with militant views about various "causes" or who challenge or obstruct such causes revived it.

Law of the Land

BLIND JUSTICE

Jurists of ancient Egypt realized very early that it is practically impossible for a judge to be unaffected by personal contacts with persons who appear before him. In an attempt to secure "blind justice," with verdicts unaffected by personalities, many trials were conducted in semidarkened rooms. The theory was that if judges couldn't see the plaintiffs and defendants, they wouldn't be affected by what they already knew about the accused.

Roman law stressed the necessity of blind justice, and this concept passed into most Western systems of jurisprudence.

One of the world's most famous statues, which was erected over Old Bailey Court in the inner city of London, shows a blindfolded justice holding scales in which to weigh the merits of cases.

In practice the ideal of blind justice has seldom been achieved. United States' efforts in this direction include not only provisions by which prejudiced judges are supposed to disqualify themselves, but also elaborate rules aimed at preventing jurors from reading newspaper accounts of activities during a trial.

TRAFFIC LAWS

Traffic laws are a natural and inevitable fruit of technicological progress. Wherever vehicles have been made in numbers sufficient to create congestion, regulations governing their use have been passed. Traffic laws, in the true sense of the word, were inaugurated in imperial Rome. By edict of the emperor, chariots were banned from the most heavily used streets except during the hours between sunset and dawn.

New Amsterdam established the first traffic law of the New World on June 27, 1652. In order to reduce accidents the council ordered that "no wagons, carts or sleighs shall be run, rode, or driven at a gallop" within the city limits. The fine for violation of this law was two pounds Flemish for the first offense, four pounds for the second, and eight pounds for the third.

Auto speed laws were first introduced in New York State in 1904. Because of a rash of accidents involving the new vehicles, speed limits were set for horseless buggies. A driver was required to stay under 10 mph in congested areas and under 15 mph in villages. On the open road, he was permitted to dash along at 20 mph.

While occupying the White House, Ulysses S. Grant (unrecognized) was arrested for exceeding the Washington speed limit in a buggy. He posted a $20 bond, failed to appear for the hearing, but wrote a letter commending the black police officer who had stopped him.

PASSPORT

Until modern times, ports located on seas and rivers were the funnels through which practically all commerce and passengers poured. Many ports were independent city-states, free to set their own regulations about who could enter the gates and pass through them to continue a journey.

An official messenger traveling on business for a ruler of Egypt was typically given a *cartouche*, or oval figure bearing the pharaoh's name in hieroglyphics. This device, which was presented to the governors of ports, constituted an imperial order that the messenger be allowed to pass.

Roman emperors issued letters of safe conduct that warned of dire consequences if the bearers were annoyed or molested by authorities of the cities through which they passed.

By the time the famous Magna Carta was drawn up in the thirteenth century, the passport had become so important that stipulations concerning its use were included in the "great charter." At that time and for several centuries afterward, most Western nations required every passport to bear the signature of the king.

The relaxation of restrictions later enabled most Europeans to go abroad without passports. But World War I brought a revival of the ancient practice. Photographs were added to British passports late in 1914; today they are universally required. In addition to the document authorizing travelers to "pass through ports," visas are needed for visits to countries behind the Iron Curtain and in many emerging nations of Africa and the Pacific.

OUTLAW

The concept of the outlaw can be traced into prehistoric civilizations. First written records are in the Bible and in secular documents produced five thousand years or so ago.

Since laws were shaped for the protection of citizens, a person no longer sheltered by society but repudiated by it was literally (not figuratively) "outside the law." To kill an outlaw was not murder, but an act that brought commendation and perhaps reward.

Now simply of historic interest in most regions of the West-

195

ern world, outlawry is still recognized in a few—in the sovereign state of North Carolina, USA, for example.

Early in 1970 a judge of Fayetteville, North Carolina, signed an order declaring three escaped prisoners to be outlaws. This meant that they were outside the protection of the law. Any citizen could try to capture them; if they resisted, they could be killed on the spot without penalty.

Many jurists insist that statutes covering outlawry should be rescinded in North Carolina—and everywhere else they still remain in force. Framed in an era when every man needed the protection of his tribe or city because of hostile persons on the outside, outlawry tenaciously retains a toehold upon Western systems of justice even in the Space Age.

CORONER'S JURY

The coroner, or representative of the crown, had only a few functions when first appointed by English sovereigns six hundred years ago.

Gradually the duties and powers of this functionary increased, however. Eventually it became a basic aspect of common law that the king's representative should inquire into every case of death in which foul play was suspected.

To assist the official, it became a standard practice to name a jury made up of half the number of persons included in a trial jury.

Transmitted to America and perpetuated when the interests of the crown (or king) were no longer involved, the coroner's jury of six persons was often chosen in quite a casual fashion. Some states still require the coroner to "empanel a jury of half a dozen bystanders" when he sifts evidence to determine whether or not death came as a result of natural causes.

STATE'S EVIDENCE

As early as the thirteenth century, many kinds of legal proceedings were considered as involving the ruler as plantiff and the accused subject as defendant. In English law, evidence for the Crown was commonly known as King's evidence—or Queen's evidence during periods when the throne was occupied by a woman.

Prosecuting attorneys very early learned that they stood a good chance of winning a case when they could persuade one of several accused of a crime to admit his guilt and testify against his accomplices. This special type of King's evidence usually involved an unwritten gentleman's agreement that the prosecution would deal lightly with the person who gave information that incriminated himself as well as others.

Transferred to the liberated colonies in America, the concept of the ruler as plaintiff was modified so that the state played that role. Whether in federal, state, or local trials an accused person who testifies against himself and his accomplices is said to have given "state's evidence."

ACT OF GOD

In struggling to deal properly with events beyond human control, jurists who framed English common law resorted to the concept of an "act of God."

Any loss caused by events that no person started or stopped —hurricanes, lightning, floods, and similar disasters—was attributed to deity. This theory fitted in nicely with the strongly Calvinistic views of many of England's leading lawyers.

No person is responsible for an injury or loss that stems from "natural forces or the enemies of the state." This principle still affects many legal decisions, though there is increasing doubt that God Almighty is directly responsible for some of the havoc visited upon mankind.

A person or corporation sued for breach of contract has a good chance of winning the case if he can show that his nonperformance stemmed from an act of God. Literal rather than figurative interpretation of the concept has prevailed in such cases as a celebrated eighteenth-century lawsuit in which a Devonshire jury found that the "Deceased died by the Act of God, brought about by the flooded condition of the river."

SPECIAL TREATMENT FOR MENTALLY DISTURBED LAWBREAKERS

Geronimo Cardano, a sixteenth-century Italian physician and mathematician, was centuries ahead of his time. Though few persons of the era paid much attention to it, he wrote an entire book aimed at establishing the legal principle of "moral insanity."

Cardano's book, which was a key force leading to the nineteenth-century laws requiring special treatment of persons suffering from mental illness, grew out of a personal tragedy.

His son, who was regarded as "strange" from boyhood, married in spite of his father's attempts to prevent the match. Within weeks after the honeymoon young Cardano poisoned his bride. Brought to trial, he was speedily convicted and beheaded.

Lifelong imprisonment in a suitable mental institution should have been the punishment, his grieving father argued.

Cardano's verbose but brilliant plea that society modify its rules when dealing with mentally disturbed lawbreakers was largely ignored in his own day. However, it set in motion the forces that produced complex laws that made a distinction between accused and condemned persons "of right mind" and those judged by experts to be incapable of being fully responsible for their own acts.

HUNTING LICENSE

Federal and state game laws had been in force for nearly a century before anyone thought of discouraging hunting by charging hunters a fee for the privilege.

Though still plentiful in many parts of New York State in the mid-nineteenth century, ranks of deer were beginning to become noticeably thinner in Suffolk County. A statute of 1864, the first of its type in the world, provided that henceforth anyone wanting to hunt deer in Suffolk County had to get official permission—and pay $10 for a hunting license.

As a concession to popular opinion, and in an effort to

persuade voters that the radical new legislation was really good, the fees collected for hunting licenses were designated to be added to the poor funds of the towns in which the licenses were issued.

DOG LICENSE

The success of the pioneer New York State law requiring deer hunters to buy licenses fostered other new legislation designed to raise revenue with a minimum of voter resistance.

One such measure was the dog license law of 1894. Prodded by the then new and controversial Society for the Prevention of Cruelty to Animals, New York legislators ruled that every dog owner—in cities over 1,200,000 (thereby exempting all citizens except residents of New York City)—should pay two dollars a year.

The florid and almost pious language of the edict stressed the fact that the reason for collecting the two-dollar fee was to "provide for the better protection of lost and strayed animals and for securing the rights of the owners thereof."

AUTO LICENSE TAGS

Having enacted legislation requiring many deer hunters and substantial numbers of dog owners to buy annual licenses, lawmakers of New York State took another pioneer step in 1901.

Every owner of a gasoline buggy was required to register his name and address, along with a description of the machine, within thirty days after April 25. A registration fee of one dollar was charged.

To make certain that no auto enthusiasts evaded the statute, it was stipulated that upon registration each machine should be equipped with a metal tag at least three inches high, bearing the initials of the owner.

During the first year that license tags were required, New York collected $954 in registration fees; in 1902, the figure jumped to a colossal $1,082.

199

ELECTROCUTION

Seeking "a humane method of dispatching the condemned," members of the New York State legislature debated a variety of alternatives during the 1880's. Practically everyone agreed that hanging was brutal and often inefficient, but it was hard to agree on an alternative.

Eventually, lawmakers pondered evidence from the journals of Benjamin Franklin. Using electric current generated by three Leyden jars, the Sage of Philadelphia had dispatched several chickens, a turkey, and a lamb. He was positive that they died without pain.

On the basis of this evidence, and on the testimony by Thomas Edison and other experts in the new science of electricity, an act providing for painless execution by means of electricity was adopted.

Dr. Alphonse D. Rockwell had invented a special chair in which a person could be strapped before the electrodes were attached. Using this device, the authorities at Auburn Prison performed the first electrocution on August 6, 1890.

Their victim was William Kemmler, who had been convicted of the brutal murder of Matilda Ziegler. Contrary to the original theory, Kemmler failed to die quickly and painlessly—but the new method of executing a condemned man seemed so much less messy than a rope or firing squad that it was retained and soon had widespread use in the United States.

BIRTH REGISTRATION

Since ancient times kings and rulers have been eager to know precisely how many subjects they governed. Consequently, a census was taken at sporadic intervals in many kingdoms. A census, ordered by the emperor of Rome, is mentioned in the New Testament in connection with the birth of Christ.

Legal requirements that births be registered—as a way of keeping running records of population figures—didn't emerge until very recent times. The first formal birth registration law was enacted by the Georgia state legislature in 1823. Clerks of the court were required to "enter and register in a permanently bound book" all births within their respective counties.

Once registration of birth became mandatory throughout the United States and some other nations, the birth certificate became a vital legal instrument necessary for establishing one's claims to a passport, social security, and other benefits.

JUVENILE COURT

Until 1899 no legal distinction was made anywhere in the world between adults and juveniles accused of crimes or misdemeanors.

United States' advocates of reform in the legal system argued during the Gay Nineties that a male or female "of tender years" should be given special treatment. Eventually the Juvenile Court of Cook County, Illinois, was established on April 21, 1899, and opened for business on July 1 of that year.

Under the impact of the Chicago experiment, most nations in the Western world have made legal distinctions between adults and juveniles, with the latter being exempt from many penalties and tried before judges who specialize in the punishment and rehabilitation of juveniles who break laws made by adults.

201

FEDERAL PROHIBITION OF NARCOTICS

Until 1909 no federal statute prohibited importation of any narcotic into the United States. Even then, the only drug covered by the law was opium.

A few states made sporadic and generally ineffective attempts to keep habit-forming drugs from coming across their borders. Many authorities, including the leading spokesmen of the medical establishment, considered it necessary that a free flow of narcotics be maintained.

So much opium was used by military doctors during the Civil War that addiction among discharged veterans reached an all-time U.S. high. Not until years after the war did the adverse effects of opium on the men who became hooked when it was administered to them in combat prod Congress into taking the first feeble step toward federal drug control.

CITIZENSHIP FOR AMERICAN INDIANS

Until this century aboriginal Americans were treated as wards of the federal government and were denied the usual rights of citizenship.

Crusaders began advocating "equal rights for the first Americans" in the aftermath of World War I. It wasn't until 1924, however, that Congress took belated action and passed legislation guaranteeing U.S. citizenship to American Indians.

Even then the Indian remained in an ambiguous situation for he was (and remains today) a citizen of both his tribe and his country. Tribal demands have frequently come into conflict with the demands of U.S. citizenship; one Navajo council formally demanded in 1969 that they be empowered to decide whether or not white-skinned U.S. citizens could come and go on Navajo land.

Nearly half a century after winning the formal right of full citizenship (even though he was born in this country—the basis for citizenship for most other Americans), the Indian remains a second-class citizen by virtue of the legal restrictions placed upon him.

Money

INTEREST

Before the beginning of recorded history some prosperous and ingenious person hit upon a novel idea. When an acquaintance borrowed goods or money from him, he charged a fee for the use of it.

Long regarded as "usury" and condemned in Scripture, the notion of charging a fee for the temporary use of capital was so vital that it refused to die. Hebrews ultimately made a neat accommodation. Usury was forbidden within the community, but carried no stigma of disapproval when outsiders or "strangers" were on the receiving end of the fiscal agreement (Deut. 23:19-20).

Greek kings and Roman emperors tried to regulate the lending of money, and several times stipulated legal ceilings for interest. In practice, there is ample evidence that the rich often managed to charge sufficient interest to reduce borrowers gradually to hopeless lifelong indebtedness—or economic slavery.

Jews were Europe's earliest and for a long time, only professional moneylenders. Their religious laws made it acceptable to practice usury, or to lend money at interest, to "outsiders" of the Christian faith. Early rulers of England borrowed heavily at high rates—then retaliated by condoning regulations under which the Jews could collect no interest from the heirs of borrowers until they reached the age of majority—or legal accountability.

For at least 3,500 years a multitude of nations, under various forms of government, have tried to control interest rates; so far no such effort has been fully successful.

BANK NOTES

Paper money, or currency, is believed to have gotten its start in China about 2600 B.C. Bearing the imprint of the emperor's treasury and printed in blue ink on paper made from the fibre of the mulberry tree, notes nearly 5,000 years old are still preserved.

Chinese officials soon found that it was awkward and cumbersome for the government to be responsible for this kind of money. As a result, individual banks printed their own "demand notes." Literally "the notes of a bank," such Chinese pieces were in circulation before the first European bank was established at Barcelona about 1401.

With the rise of private banking in the Western world, the custom of printing notes for which the banks assumed responsibility became practically universal.

Now, however, such notes have been replaced by currency issued by governments. But the term "bank note" is so firmly entrenched in speech that it is still used to label paper money for which no bank has any responsibility.

CHECK

During the seventeenth and eighteenth centuries, the growing size of commercial transactions made it awkward and frequently dangerous to transfer funds in gold and silver.

No one knows when or where some businessman hit upon the idea of preparing a bill of exchange payable by his banker to a specified person or to the bearer. Once the concept was devised it spread rapidly and was soon common throughout western Europe.

As a safety measure, early bills of exchange carried counterfoils which were separated from the drafts themselves at the time they were paid. Bankers retained these counterfoils, or indents, as a check to alteration or forgery.

Beginning about 1800, the importance of the check retained by a bank caused its name to be attached to the draft validated by it. By 1882 the English Parliament felt it necessary to give the fiscal instrument and its name statutory definition as "a bill of exchange drawn on a banker payable on demand."

Until recent times prankish checkwriters have been able to utilize practically any material that will convey writing or engraving: scraps of notepaper, leather, and even slabs of metal.

With the rise of automated banking came the electric eye, which requires a code number that can be scanned accurately and quickly. As a result the blank or "counter" check, and the check written on whatever material strikes the user's fancy, have become obsolete. Today, few banks process any checks except those which bear identification numbers imprinted on the blanks.

GUINEA

Travelers to England often find themselves puzzled by the fact that even under the new decimal system of coinage, merchants of the island kingdom often price merchandise in terms of a coin that doesn't exist: the guinea.

This state of affairs stems from the days of King Charles II. During his reign, a gold coin (first struck in 1663) was dubbed a guinea because it was made of gold brought from the Guinea coast of Africa.

The original guinea was valued at one pound or twenty shillings. But silver coins of the era were depreciating while the value of gold was rising. At one period a guinea was worth thirty shillings. Later, in 1717, its value was fixed by parliament at twenty-one shillings (just a fraction more than one pound).

No guineas have been coined since 1813. Most of those still in existence are in the hands of collectors. In spite of the fact that the coin has been out of circulation for about 150 years, tradesmen of Britain cling to the custom of pricing some merchandise in guineas rather than in pounds.

DIME

Only the United States has a coin called a dime. Its use in vending machines and coin telephones makes it one of the most important pieces of metal money in this country. The annual production of dimes has averaged more than one million pieces since 1960; so far, the all-time record year was 1966 in which 3,196,000,000 dimes were issued by the mints.

Gouverneur Morris is responsible for existence of the coin. A skilled linguist, Morris remembered that medieval churchmen were accustomed to paying a tithe (10 percent) of their income to the church. Widely called *dyme*, this practice was so well established that it appears in John Wycliffe's translation of the Bible (Genesis 14:20).

Morris recommended to the Continental Congress that the proposed new coinage system include a ten-cent piece to be called by the French term for tithe. American lawmakers adopted the idea for the coin and the name, but by the mint act of 1792 specified that it should be spelled *dime*.

MILLED EDGES ON COINS

During eras when gold and silver coins circulated freely, many persons made a practice of filing off a bit of precious metal from each coin that passed through their hands. Bold rogues even clipped money, removing relatively large chunks from coins and then passing them along at face value.

Both to protect coins from wear and to prevent fraudulent removal of their valuable metal, French machinist Antoine Boucher devised a way to stamp coins with raised borders and grooved or "milled" edges.

Boucher's sixteenth-century invention quickly went international. England struck its first coins with milled edges in 1553, but found the manufacturing process so expensive that it was, for a time, abandoned. When an increase in filing and clipping created a situation in which a gold or silver coin might lose one-forth its weight within a few months after being issued, the practice of milling coins became standard in England in 1662.

Some rogues tried to devise a way to clip coins, then provide the new discs with counterfeit edges. When Oliver Cromwell rose to power he suggested that pious mottoes around the edges of coins would be harder to counterfeit than milling. His idea didn't work very well, so he had some coins struck with the message: "The Penalty for Clipping This Coin Is Death."

Today's coins are made entirely of base metals, and aren't worth clipping. But milled edges are so firmly entrenched that they are commonly used by mints of most nations.

CENT

Gouverneur Morris, whose ideas carried a great deal of weight in the Continental Congress, wanted coins of the new nation to be "of wide range in value, for the better promotion of commerce."

In a letter dated April 30, 1783, he outlined a list of useful denominations but gave names to only a few of them. It took two years for the Congress to agree on a plan in which the monetary unit of the United States would be the dollar. A second provision stipulated that the smallest coin should be one of copper, "of which 200 shall pass for one dollar." Finally, the Act of July 6, 1785, provided that "the several pieces shall increase in a decimal ratio."

That last stipulation created difficulties in carrying out the idea of producing a coin worth .005 dollar. So in August of the same year Congress adopted a system of coinage ranging from the Gold Eagle ($10) to the cent ($.01). Two and one-fourth pounds of copper, avoirdupois, were stipulated to be equal to one hundred cents.

Though half-cent coins were later coined and used for a time, they proved unsatisfactory. As a result the copper piece whose name stems from Latin for "one one-hundredth" became the backbone of small-time commerce and much later became very important when bargains were priced at one cent below an even number of dollars.

Born as a result of a compromise between competing systems of currency, the one-cent piece remains perennially important. In 1969, 5,687 million of them were produced.

"FASCIST SYMBOL" ON DIME

During World War I, while fighting on the side of the Allies, Benito Mussolini adopted as the symbol of his movement the *fasces* (bundle of rods enclosing a protruding ax) used as the emblem of authority in ancient Rome. Mussolini was then relatively obscure and the fascist movement he founded was not to take form for years.

Without any knowledge of events in Italy, coin designer Adolph Weinman suggested a design for a new U.S. dime to replace the old Liberty-head piece that had long been in circulation. Because the fasces is a classical symbol of authority, Weinman suggested that it would be a fitting design for the reverse of the new coin that would portray the head of Mercury, a Roman god, on its frontside.

Adopted in 1916, three years before the first organizational meeting of Mussolini's blackshirts, the new coin attracted only admiration until fascism surged into the news. Though bombarded for many years with demands that use of the fasces on the dime be dropped, the U.S. Treasury Department retained the symbol, even after the face of Franklin D. Roosevelt replaced that of Mercury on the obverse side of the coin in 1946.

NICKEL

Formerly all-important as "king of the 5-and-10-cent store," the nickel began its life as the half-dime.

Five-cent pieces were first minted by the U.S. Government in 1794. Intended to facilitate commerce, these earliest half-dimes were made entirely of silver. As the price of the precious metal rose, the production of the silver pieces declined but was not suspended until 1873.

Meanwhile, metallurgists had discovered that a much cheaper substance, harder than silver but having some super-ficial resemblance to it, was becoming more abundant. In 1866 the U.S. mint began issuing half-dimes made of nickel.

Gradually the name of the metal replaced that of the older coin and *nickel* came into universal use to designate a half-dime. During the first seventy-five years they were made, nickels were the most popular of U.S. coins. More than two billion of them were struck and most remained in circulation for many years.

Today's nickel isn't really nickel; instead it is a complex compound of several metals. In 1965 the mint issued 2,016 million nickels—more than the total number struck between 1866 and 1940.

"ALMIGHTY DOLLAR"

Alexander Hamilton, who played a decisive role in shaping U.S. monetary policies, felt that the dollar would be the most important of all coins. Consequently he insisted that both gold and silver pieces be coined.

In the Act of 1792, Congress authorized the mint to make

silver dollars—but no gold ones were struck until discovery of gold made the precious metal abundant.

Notes of the Continental Congress entitled the bearer to receive Spanish milled dollars "or the value thereof in gold or silver." In spite of the fact that this promise proved to be worthless, the same policy was followed with paper dollars bearing the imprint of the U.S. Government.

So many dollars of various kinds were in circulation by the end of the eighteenth century that Hamilton's prediction proved to be correct.

Washington Irving is generally credited with having coined the contemptuous label "almighty dollar." The first known printed use of the term was in a story by Irving published in *The New Yorker.* Comparing the Creoles of Louisiana with dollar-eager businessmen from the east, Irving (mistakenly) reported that "the almighty dollar, that great object of universal devotion throughout our land, seems to have no genuine devotees in these peculiar villages."

WAR BONDS

Interest-bearing bonds, sold for the express purpose of financing military operations, were launched in the United States in 1812.

That year, political leaders clearly saw that money received from taxes wouldn't be adequate to buy military equipment that experts said the nation would need for "an inevitable conflict with Great Britain."

Bonds in the amount of $11 million—sufficient to pay for only a few hours' conflict in Vietnam—were issued on March 14, 1812. With this fiscal support in hand Congress declared war on Great Britain just two months and two days after taking steps to buy more guns and other equipment.

Five other special "war bond" issues were floated before the War of 1812 drew to a close. In every subsequent military conflict, the U.S. Government has relied heavily upon the sale of war bonds to finance men fighting on land, on the sea, in the air, and under the sea.

211

TWO BITS

Though English, French, and Spanish coins continued to circulate in the early years of U.S. independence, the supply of these pieces combined with the output of the mint was inadequate to meet the demand.

Spanish dollars, made of an extremely soft type of silver, were easily cut into fragments or "bits." Typically, such a coin was cut into eight bits which were used as small change in commercial transactions.

Two such bits, or a single piece roughly one-fourth the size of a Spanish dollar, were treated as equal in value to the U.S. twenty-five cent piece. So many pieces of cut silver circulated for so long that when use of the two-bit piece ceased the name "two bits" clung to the quarter-dollar.

GREENBACK

Within weeks after the outbreak of the Civil War, Abraham Lincoln and his advisors faced a major crisis. The supply of specie (gold and silver coins) plus certificates that could be exchanged for gold at any bank was inadequate to finance the war. There simply wasn't enough of this kind of money to pay the troops—to say nothing of outfitting them and providing weapons.

There was only one course to take, fiscal experts agreed.

The Union Government would have to issue a huge supply of paper money of a new kind. Persons who accepted this money would not be under the delusion that it could be exchanged for gold at will.

Because the new money was printed with green ink on the back, it was almost inevitable that the bills should immediately be called greenbacks.

The first issue of greenbacks, in April, 1862, bypassed the $1 bill; denominations of notes issued were: $5, $10, $20, $50, $100, $500, and $1,000.

The greenbacks depreciated rapidly. Within two years the business world was treating $2.84 in greenbacks as equivalent to one dollar in gold. Because the production of wartime paper money was seldom halted even briefly, greenbacks depreciated in relation to the cost of rent, commodities, and services.

In spite of this severe early warning, the United States' production of greenbacks (no longer even theoretically backed by gold) has kept printing presses working twenty-four hours a day, seven days a week. Paper currency in circulation in the United States in 1950 amounted to about $35,314 million. Twenty years later, the total exceeded $57 billion.

"IN GOD WE TRUST"

Late in 1861 a Maryland farmer wrote a letter to Salmon P. Chase, U.S. Secretary of the Treasury. As citizens of a Christian nation, the farmer urged, Americans should give recognition to the Deity on the most universally used everyday articles, namely, coins and currency.

Chase pondered the idea, consulted other national leaders, and concluded that in the heated climate of the Civil War such a religious motto would be an invaluable boost to morale. He wrote the director of the mint at Philadelphia, urging that coins should "express in the fewest words the conviction that no nation can be strong except in the strength of God."

Congressional action came in April, 1864, in the form of an authorization empowering the director of the mint to fix the shape, mottoes, and devices judged appropriate. "In God

213

We Trust" first appeared on the two-cent piece of 1864—now a rare collector's item.

In spite of the clamor from groups contending that use of the inscription violates the concept of separation of church and state, on July 11, 1955, Congress enacted legislation providing that "all United States currency and coins shall bear the inscription 'In God We Trust.' "

Last Things

LAST WILL AND TESTAMENT

No one knows precisely what portion of the world's wealth is, for all practical purposes, controlled by the dead, but the percentage is very substantial. Trust funds, foundations, and other agencies for directing the use of one's assets for generations or even centuries after death have proliferated in modern times.

As a legal device, the "last will and testament" is a comparatively modern invention. It is rooted, however, in practices that predate the beginning of recorded history.

Attempts to carry out the expressed wishes of the dead regarding the property they had left were faithfully made by their survivors. Especially in cases involving kings and rulers, such obedience often required decades of work after a member of royalty had died. Extending downward in the social and political hierarchy, similar attitudes began to be reflected in the attention to pre-death wishes of persons of wealth and power even if they were not heads of state.

By the time the Roman Empire dominated most of the known world, it was a common practice for persons of all rank to give directions about the disposal of the property they owned. The freedom to do this on the part of individuals was in striking contrast with the rigid social rules that had dictated the disposition of lands and titles as late as the time of the Old Testament patriarchs.

At least in theory, a present-day will is binding "for all time." The elaborate conditions attached to some bequests make it impossible to administer them; great numbers of institutions in the United States have trust funds and endowments that are so restricted that their income cannot be spent.

CLOSING THE EYES OF THE DEAD

Subtle kinds of fear rather than respect probably led to development of the practically universal practice of closing the eyes of the dead. Already very old when the book of Genesis was written (see Genesis 46:4), the custom was linked with even older concepts of "the evil eye." To be glanced upon by the eye of a dead man, traditions of many cultures assert, is to risk an attack by demons—or even sudden death.

There was but one way to make sure that the eyes of the dead would not bring evil to those who prepared their bodies and kept vigil in the period before burial. That method sounds simpler than it is: simply close the eyes.

During the hours after death the muscles become increasingly rigid; after twelve hours it is difficult to change the position or appearance of a corpse. This means that a person who dies with his eyes wide open and isn't found for many hours poses special problems.

Various small household articles have been widely used as weights to close the eyes of the dead. In England, the large copper penny was just the right size and weight for use in final rites. As a result the closing of a dead man's eyes with

216

pennies (bigger and heavier than the U.S. one-cent piece) prevailed for centuries. It was so very common that in spite of the fact that the practice itself has disappeared, the label "a person who would steal coppers from dead men's eyes" is still applied to the lowest kind of thief.

TO GO WEST

Prehistoric religious views in which sun-worship was a major motif set the stage for verbal formulas suggesting that the soul of a dead person goes to the west rather than to the north, south, or east.

Since the sun seemed to "die" every evening when it set in the west, it was natural—even inevitable—that souls of humans should be depicted as traveling in this direction. Worldwide in scope and found among cultures that have little else in common, the notion of the west as the abode of the dead prevailed among ancient Egyptians, Greeks, American Indians, and inhabitants of remote Pacific islands.

Norsemen were so sure that the soul travels west that arrangements for funerals of dignitaries were planned accordingly. Upon the death of a Viking chieftain, his body was placed in a boat with the sails set in such fashion that it was calculated to transport him "into the setting sun."

Folk tales that link the origin of the emphasis upon "going west" with American migration toward the western frontier are modern in origin.

DEATH MASKS

In order to preserve the features of rulers and heroes, citizens of ancient Mediterranean city-states learned how to make impressions, or masks, during the hours immediately after a famous person died. Many such masks were made of gold or silver; substantial numbers of them are preserved in museums.

Late in the Middle Ages, some unknown craftsman—probably but not certainly a workman in a pottery—hit upon a

217

radical idea. By using soft clay that would gradually harden, he ought to be able to reproduce features even more effectively than with precious metals.

Gradually perfected and revolutionized, using plaster of Paris rather than ordinary potter's clay, the art of making death masks was highly regarded until quite recent times.

The world's most famous waxworks—Madame Tussaud's in London—owes its existence to the importance of the death mask. During the French Revolution a young woman with nimble fingers was required to make death masks of many victims of the guillotine. She later fled to England, took her skill with her, and in lieu of plaster masks began making wax models of heads. Expanded to involve the skillful reproduction of entire bodies, the "wax museum" that developed from her representation of dead notables is one of the world's prime tourist attractions.

EMBALMING

Preservation of the bodies of dead rulers and notables originated in Egypt at least six thousand years ago. Reverence, respect, love, and strong beliefs about the afterlife were among the motives that brought the practice into being.

Even in predynastic periods the earliest Egyptians often wrapped their dead in linen and then covered the bodies with goatskins to protect them from the soil. Burial in subterranean chambers came later. Increasingly elaborate attempts to preserve bodies had their beginning about 4000 B.C.

According to the Greek historian Herodotus, by the fifth century B.C., Egyptians had several modes of embalming. The most expensive cost about $1,125; a middle-class preparation for burial ran to about $375; even the poor could afford the low cost of perfunctory embalming.

Good work in those days involved removing the viscera and drawing the brain out through the nostrils without causing defacement. After being washed with palm wine, body cavities were filled with pine, myrrh, pounded cinnamon, and other spices.

By the nineteenth century, modern embalming had had its start. After the blood vessels of a corpse were emptied, alcohol or ether was injected to remove body fat. Then tannic acid was used as a preservative.

It wasn't until formaldehyde became common and inexpensive, early in this century, that honest-to-goodness "preservation" of intact bodies became feasible.

KNELL

Various kinds of bells made from a variety of materials developed independently in European, Oriental, and "primitive" cultures. Though they have played a variety of roles, all bells in all cultures have one important trait in common: their noise is especially effective in driving away evil spirits. At least, that has been the practically universal belief.

With the rise of Christianity, inherited customs such as the ringing of bells for the dead and dying were gradually modified. A special pattern of sounds, instantly understood by all who grew up in cultures where it was used, was indicated by the ringing of "the passing bell." Ostensibly a signal asking all Christians to pray for the soul of a person about to leave his mortal body, it was still widely regarded as "an instrument to drive away the evil spirits who stood at the bed of the dying, ready to seize their prey."

A later and more elaborate modification of the ringing of the passing bell produced the pattern of sounds that became known as the "knell." This indicated death, and served as a public announcement.

Accosted by an acquaintance whose ear was caught by the sounding of a knell and asked the name of the man who had died, John Donne pondered the incident and from it wrote his world-famous lines "For whom the bell tolls."

Even though many cathedrals and churches still have great bells, few persons are skillful enough to use them to ring a knell. Hence this once universal custom is now observed only rarely in the United States, in connection with the death of a president or national hero.

219

WAKE

From the earliest recorded times it has been customary for friends and relatives to sit up all night with the body of a deceased loved one. Love and reverence were ingredients in the compound that led to development of this practice, but they were not dominant.

It was widely feared that unless a careful watch was kept, an evil spirit might enter the body before funeral ceremonies were completed. Relatives who found the job of guarding a corpse burdensome often secured paid mourners; this practice is referred to in numerous ancient documents. Scriptural emphasis upon mourners (mentioned dozens of times) shows that in Israel the loud cries or wails of the mourners were very important. These sounds simultaneously indicated mourning and kept demons away. Among the Hebrews, professional mourners were called both "singing women" (2 Chronicles 35:25) and "cunning women" (Jeremiah 9:17).

Anglo-Saxons who maintained the custom of keeping vigils with the dead gave us the modern term "wake." Partly because too many wakes were marked by excessive drinking, partly because the professional undertaker has assumed many functions long linked with sorrowing ones, the full-fledged wake is rapidly vanishing. In many U.S. communities, though, friends and loved ones still strive to maintain an "honor guard" by the side of a corpse in an abbreviated daylight version of the ancient wake.

FUNERAL MARCH

During eras when Europe was largely dominated by cities of 20,000 to 50,000 population, the death of a local notable called for a massive turnout at final rites. Partly to help pallbearers to work in unison, composers began writing special "dead marches" in slow tempo.

Music of this sort contrasted vividly with the brisk tempo of the widely used "military marches."

The importance of the funeral march was so great that

several famous composers, notably Georg Friedrich Händel and Ludwig van Beethoven, lent their talents to this special type of music. Shakespeare's plays include numerous references to it.

In modern times the most popular of all funeral marches is a sonata by Frédéric Chopin. Taken from his Opus 35, the composition, which is used during the final rites honoring the head of a government, was not originally designed to express grief at the death of an individual. Chopin wrote it to lament the loss of the independence of Poland, but the sonata proved so potent in transcending cultural barriers and expressing "grief too deep for words" that it has long served as *the* funeral march of the Western world.

RIGHT-OF-WAY BY FUNERAL PROCESSION

Traffic-choked modern cities are having increasing difficulty with the hoary tradition of a funeral procession having the right-of-way over all other traffic. Here the weight of custom is clearly visible, for there are few statutes actually requiring traffic to halt at the approach of a funeral procession.

Legal factors are seldom involved even when a modern funeral procession is led by an off-duty police officer in uniform or by a deputized and uniformed member of a special "escort service." In practically all cities and towns motorists who wish

221

to do so can ignore a funeral procession by cutting through or passing it without risk of penalty.

This special way of showing respect for the dead is so deeply entrenched, however, that in a great many modern communities all traffic halts in order to permit funeral processions to proceed without interruption.

The ancient inhabitants of northern Europe were convinced that it was positively dangerous to cause even a brief halt in the movement of a corpse to the grave. A stop, insisted many a tale in Norse mythology, provided an opportunity for the ghost of the deceased to make an escape. Once it got away there was no way to capture it and inter it with the body it had inhabited.

It was fear—that waned as respect for the dead mounted—that created a climate in which tradition so strongly decreed that a funeral procession must have the right-of-way that for practical purposes the custom was (and is) treated as legally binding.

GOD'S ACRE

At least as early as the tenth century, the inhabitants of Britain were referring to any well-defined piece of tilled land by a title that emerged into modern speech as "acre."

For centuries, the acre was merely "a field" or "a piece of land" whose size was not specified.

The founders of English villages typically set aside specific plots of ground for the burial of the dead. An English-style stone fence, a row of trees, or a brook might serve as a boundary of such a field. It didn't belong to any individual—or even to the community. So there was but one thing to call it: "God's acre."

The size of the acre was first defined by royal decree in the thirteenth century, during the rule of King Edward I, as the quantity of land a yoke of oxen can plow in a day. King Henry VIII modified the description to "a piece of land 40 poles long by 4 broad" (4,840 square yards).

King Henry's acre has survived into modern times as a precise and all-important unit of measurement in Britain and the United States. But the much older "piece of land" with definite boundaries but no specific size is meant when a burial ground is called by the once literal term "God's acre."

THREE VOLLEYS OVER THE GRAVE

Noise-making devices, ranging from cattle horns to drums and (among the Chinese) firecrackers, have been employed for centuries as part of the ritual for burial. Practically all scholars agree that the original purpose of these noises was to drive away the spirit of the dead person so that he would not hover about to haunt the living.

Once guns had been invented and perfected, the sounds made by them so overshadowed all others that the practice of firing them at the time of interment became general.

Positive documentary evidence is lacking, but many incidental references in early accounts suggest that the influence of the Holy Trinity caused the number of volleys to be fixed at three rather than one, four, or more.

Three volleys were fired over the graves of men, women, and children alike as late as the sixteenth century. Largely through pressure by the military establishments of major European countries, the indiscriminate firing of guns at the graveside was discontinued. Today they sound only during the burial of a person (male or female) who has served honorably in the armed forces—but the influence of tradition is so great that the veterans who raise their rifles to fire the blank cartridges still fire precisely three volleys.

FUNERAL DIRECTOR

Friends and relatives who had the requisite skills but didn't serve as professionals often prepared bodies for burial in ancient times. This was the case with Jesus of Nazareth.

Long before he was born, however, priests especially trained for the task "made ready" the bodies of pharaohs, kings, and persons of wealth. Their functions were reserved for members of the religious establishment until the spread of Christianity fostered the rise of secular professionals who got the dead ready for interment.

Gradually the role of these workers with the dead expanded. Funeral arrangements themselves remained the province of the church until after the Protestant Reformation. It wasn't until the seventeenth century that the persons who carried out all arrangements for funerals, or undertook the grim business of embalming the bodies and arranging for services and burial, came to be called undertakers.

Like all titles with unpleasant connotations this one refused to remain stable. In an attempt to get away from the old associations linked with "undertaker" and later with "mortician," an enterprising American coined a new title. Charles E. Carter, Jr., of Washington, D.C., boldly offered his services as "funeral director" in the era after the Civil War. It wasn't until 1896, however, that the new title for a function as old as man first appeared in print.

CREMATION

As a way of disposing of the dead without losing the use of vast tracts of land, cremation came into vogue in India many centuries ago. To this day, special funeral piles or *ghats* burn almost continuously along the banks of the Ganges. The ashes are customarily scattered in the waters of the sacred river.

For a long time Europeans were aghast at the idea of burning the body of any person—except a witch or a condemned felon.

Honoretta Pratt, the wife of the Treasurer of Ireland, is believed to have been the first European to espouse cremation. In keeping with the specific orders she had given before her death on September 20, 1769, the body of the highborn woman was burned and her ashes were interred in "the new burying ground adjoining to Tyburn turnpike."

Partly as a concession to the once prevailing public opinion, statutes still make it difficult—and expensive—to cremate the dead in some states. Partly because cities are running out of burial ground, and partly because cremation appeals to moderns in a way it didn't to their great-grandparents, this method of disposing of the dead has been gaining in popularity ever since Mrs. Pratt gave it respectability in the Western world.

EPITAPH

Inscriptions commemorating their victories and reciting their triumphs constituted the epitaphs of ancient rulers—who tried to make sure they wouldn't be forgotten before ordinary persons had any means to perpetuate their memory.

Many early epitaphs were written by courtiers, then carefully carved in stone. Some kings who wanted to be sure they weren't forgotten had memorial pillars, complete with epitaphs, erected while they lived.

During classical times the value of a good epitaph was so great that a class of professional epitaph-writers was created. It was in this period, too, that enlightened persons began to realize that an epitaph that was included in a piece of great literature was likely to last longer than one inscribed upon a monument.

With the development of machines for cutting letters into stone, the epitaph went through an era of wild proliferation.

225

Some were sentimental to the point of being maudlin. Others were matter-of-fact, reciting the campaigns of English military men almost in the fashion that conquests of Babylonian and Assyrian conquerors were listed on their memorial stones.

Flippant, facetious, and humorous epitaphs are modern in origin. Many that are included in compilations are mythical, but some are authentic. A memorial stone in Putnam, Connecticut, says of Phineas G. Wright, who died in 1918 at age 89: "*Going, But Know Not Where.*"

Rising costs plus the crowding of burial grounds is rapidly making the epitaph—sentimental or silly—a thing of the past.

MOURNING BANDS

The wearing of a black band (usually around the left sleeve of one's coat) as a symbol of mourning is still rather common in Europe and in big U.S. cities with large numbers of second-generation Americans.

Such a band seems to represent the last lingering survival of once universal practices which linked black with death.

As late as the sixteenth century it was an unwritten law that when a person died, every member of his household should wear black clothing for a suitable period. This proved increasingly expensive and troublesome as merchant princes and other men of wealth created larger and larger household establishments.

Eventually many upper-class families in England and in Germany decided to compromise with tradition. Intead of going to the expense of outfitting dozens of servants in black, heirs began requiring liveried male servants to wear black gloves, black hatbands, and black crepe around their sleeves. Women wore "full mourning" attire much longer, then abandoned it rather suddenly.

Black gloves and black hatbands were gradually abandoned, but the black band about the left sleeve of a male who mourns the loss of a relative, friend, or employer has survived into the Space Age. Tradition requires that a properly respectful mourning band be about three and a fourth inches wide, and sewn around the left sleeve midway between elbow and shoulder.

TOMBSTONE

Tombstones were used at least six thousand years ago—and probably much earlier. Many of them were rounded boulders that could be rolled across the mouth of a natural cave or an artificial tomb. Some were placed directly above graves that had been dug in the ground.

Regardless of the size or precise placement of the earliest tombstones, their function was complex. They simultaneously prevented the souls of the dead from escaping, and made it difficult or impossible for grave robbers to steal trinkets, utensils, and jewelry with which the bodies of the dead were adorned.

Stones resting at the head of a grave and bearing inscriptions with information about the dead, and invitations that passersby pray for their souls, did not become common until recent centuries. With the rapid expansion of "memorial parks" from which conventional tombstones are barred, these traditional markers stemming from ancient beliefs are diminishing in importance. If present trends continue, long before the year A.D. 2500 the practice of erecting them will be abandoned, and the only tombstones in the United States will be those inherited from the past.

Bibliography

Much of the information on which this volume is based came from highly specialized sources. The American Automobile Association and numerous other associations provided answers to questions. Historical libraries in the United States and abroad were especially cooperative. In addition to technical and specialized volumes, the following works proved of special value:

Asimov, Isaac. *Realm of Measure*. Boston: Houghton Mifflin, 1960.

Brewer, Ebenezer C. *Brewer's Dictionary of Phrase and Fable*. Revised by John Freeman. 8th revised ed. New York: Harper & Row, 1964.

Carruth, Gorton, *et al.*, editors. *The Encyclopedia of American Facts and Dates*. 5th ed. New York: Thomas Y. Crowell, 1970.

Carter, Ernest F., editor. *Dictionary of Inventions and Discoveries*. New York: International Publications Service, 1969.

Friedberg, Jack, editor. *Paper Money of the United States*. 6th ed. New York: Coin & Currency Institute, 1968.

Harper, Howard V. *Days and Customs of All Faiths*. New York: Fleet Publishing Company, 1957.

Inglis, Brian. *A History of Medicine*. Cleveland: World, 1965.

Iversen, William. *O the Times! O the Manners!* New York: William Morrow, 1965.

Jewkes, John, *et al. The Sources of Invention*. 2nd ed. New York: W. W. Norton, 1970.

Kane, Joseph Nathan. *Facts About the Presidents*. 2nd. ed. New York: H. W. Wilson, 1968.

——. *Famous First Facts*. 3rd ed. New York: H. W. Wilson, 1964.

Knowlson, Thomas S. *The Origins of Popular Superstitions and Customs*. Detroit: Gale Research Associates, 1968.

Koestler, Arthur. *The Act of Creation*. Danube Edition Series. New York: The Macmillan Company, 1970.

Kull, Irving S. and Nell M. *An Encyclopedia of American History: Enlarged and Updated.* New York: Popular Library, 1965.

Kybalova, Ludmila, *et al. The Pictorial Encyclopedia of Fashion.* Trans. Claudio Rosoux. New York: Crown Publishers, 1968.

Maple, Eric. *Superstition and the Superstitious.* London: W. H. Allen, 1971.

Margotta, Roberto. *The Story of Medicine.* London: Paul Hamlyn, 1968.

Oxford English Dictionary. 13 vols. Ed. J. A. H. Murray *et al.* Oxford: The Clarendon Press, 1933.

Rapport, Samuel and Helen Wright, editors. *Great Adventures in Medicine.* Rev. ed. New York: The Dial Press, 1961.

Sepharial [pseud.]. *The Book of Charms and Talismans.* Hackensack, N. J.: Wehman Brothers, n. d.

Stewart, George R. *Names on the Land.* New York: Random House, 1945.

Stimpson, George. *A Book About American History.* New York: Harper & Row, 1956.

Taton, René. *Reason and Chance in Scientific Discovery.* Trans. A. J. Pomerans. New York: Philosophical Library, 1957.

Walsh, William S. *Curiosities of Popular Customs.* Philadelphia: J. B. Lippincott, 1897.

—————. *Handy-Book of Curious Information.* Detroit: Gale Research Associates, 1970.

Wason, Betty. *Cooks, Gluttons & Gourmets: A History of Cookery.* New York: Doubleday & Company, 1962.

Williams, Neville. *Chronology of the Modern World.* Rev. ed. New York: David McKay, 1969.

Index

233